Prothesis: Losing Myself to Find Him is a beautiful book that depicts the journey of a young woman to her true purpose and identity. By sharing her quest for meaning and a purposeful life, McKenna Vietti shows us that self-discovery is only possible as part of knowing God. Letting go of our own plans, dreams, and expectations and letting God direct our lives and shape our hearts is the key to becoming and living in harmony with our true selves. This book is a powerful reminder that being is before doing and, in the doing, we find the being.

—**Hadassah Treu**, author of *Draw Near: How Painful Experiences Become the Birthplace of Blessings*, speaker, artist, award-winning blogger and writer at onthewaybg.com.

Through sincere stories of unrealized dreams, unexpected loss, and the unpredictability of young adult life, McKenna gently and genuinely shares her journey of discovering true and lasting purpose... the same purpose we are all desperately seeking, are invited to, and can claim ourselves.

—**Cimber Cummings**, speaker, ministry director, and author of *twenty something: the things you wish someone told you about your twenties*.

Prothesis

Losing Myself to Find Him

McKenna Vietti

CALLA PRESS
PUBLISHING

Prothesis: Losing Myself to Find Him

Copyright @ 2024 by McKenna Vietti
   Published by Calla Press Publishing
   Texas Countryside
   United States 76401

Cover Design: Publisher of Calla Press Publishing
First Printing, 2024
Printed in the United States of America

All Scripture quotations, unless otherwise indicated, are taken from the Holy Bible, New International Version®, NIV®. Copyright @1973, 1978, 1984, 2011 by Biblica, Inc.™ Used by permission of Zondervan. All rights reserved worldwide. www.zondervan.com The "NIV" and "New International Version" are trademarks registered in the United States Patent and Trademark Office by Biblica, Inc.™

All emphases in Scripture quotations have been added by the author.

Trade paperback ISBN: 979-8-9888702-9-6

To Mom, who gave me a love for words and the Word.
And to Dad, who inspired me to write my own.

Contents

Introduction

Not too long ago, I stood inside a small church on a warm spring morning and felt the hard exterior that encased my heart slowly begin to break. My heart has been broken many times—over many things—but never so purposefully or beautifully as when Jesus was involved.

In this instance, the source was the chorus to a song I'd never heard or sung before; the lyrics went something like this:

Hallelujah, you have saved me. So much better this way.

I hadn't been so moved in months. It was a good thing.

But it also showed me that—despite having written and rewritten and praying over these pages that unveil the last ten years of my life—I still have so much to learn.

When I look back on some of the earliest dreams for my life, the word that especially comes to mind is *adventure*. Back then, my notion of living a full life meant traveling the globe, meeting and befriending beautiful people who lived among broken cultures, and experiencing worlds that I could later document into an exciting history. I imagined myself chasing elephants, hopping helicopters to catch last minute assignments, and diving crystal blue waters of the deep. There were other dreams too, I suppose; but they had little to do with self-sacrifice and a little more to do with self-promotion.

Those early dreams were delicate, like breath-blown glass ready to shatter beneath a burning Middle Eastern sun. Delicate, but also moldable, like clay in the hands of a Potter whose plans would emerge from the kiln with more beauty than my delicate hands could form.

The youthful, hopeful ambitions sailed from a world of saltwater reverie, but shipwrecked as I slowly came to understand that life was so much more than chasing adventures. The realization unfolded to me in small moments throughout my teenage years and later young adulthood. It began as a whisper; a quiet murmur that would beckon me to sail a different direction that was less smooth and called me to navigate more turbulent waters. In the crash of the waves, I could hear deeper a voice calling to me, although I wasn't exactly sure what it said.

Though the message was muddled, I felt prompted to change the way I approached life and determined what I was supposed to do.

Who am I supposed to be?

I had no idea.

My lack of answers saturated me in fear, hitting me over and over like waves that slam into the cliffs of a rocky coast.

When we're young, sometimes all we can think about is becoming someone else. There is an unspoken urge to grasp that golden future that weaves a tapestry of pain's past, ensuring us that if we do, we will finally be happy. After all, what other purpose does pain serve? If we cannot unravel threads that twist the design, will the result be as beautiful?

Sometimes learning to live with the pain and ugliness that life produces creates something better than we were originally hoping.

Somewhere along the way, through furious seas and tangled tapestries, I seemed to have not only lost my definition of dreams but also myself. Winds blew doors closed and people drifted out of my life. My voyage began with steady souls who held hands over my own as I steered the helm; but as the current inexorably pulled me toward an unknown destination, it seemed I was left to navigate alone.

The dreamer in me thought a life worth living meant traveling to the broken places of creation. But God showed me I didn't have to travel far at all to know brokenness. My journey morphed into a far better adventure that could, maybe someday, reach an even greater number of people.

This book is about that journey. It showcases those less than glamorous (but nonetheless dramatic) moments of feeling simultaneously lost and incomplete. As the waters grew rough, they also became blurred, almost as if I'd capsized and was drowning beneath the waves. Those moments felt just as breathless. Even other moments where I knew life was a gift, it felt as meaningless as chasing after the wind (Eccles. 2:11).

More than anything, this book is about what God taught me through a voyage that seemed to have no port of disembarkation.

I certainly don't have all the answers. We're traveling the same dirt road, feet shuffling as dust clouds drift behind us, trudging toward a destination that glimmers hope. It promises rest. It refreshes us with the truth. It assures us with the peace of mind that all along the road was necessary. When we spend seasons traveling dusty roads, all we may dream about is a well when a river is waiting for us. It may not be what we expect or what we've dreamed about, but when God has promised water, we know whatever is waiting is far better than what we were hoping for or expecting.

Mine is a road designed of both dirt and gold, of loss and disappointments; waiting out the mourning, rebuilding, re-growing, and redeeming. Time after time, the road bends back to the Creator when hopes and dreams dissipate into dust. The pages that follow are just the steps I've taken, the trails I've had to create, the routes I've had to remake. More than anything, it's what I've learned about my Lord and who he says I am. It's not just the simple words, but the truth he breathed life into, the script that has the power to penetrate hearts and change lives.

This book is for you because this journey is to be shared. I know I am not alone in the questioning and the wandering. Who else is struggling with knowing what they want? Who else feels as if they have no direction or purpose or even hope? Or maybe you feel as if you really don't know yourself at all, as I once did. Even if you are a believer, you still feel as if there are things that just don't make sense. We tend to think that if God is who he says he is and he really is enough, we shouldn't feel so empty and lost all the time. Sometimes we believe our humanness gives us the right to question the God of the universe and wonder why he doesn't just give us what we want already; in the wandering we forget that he be-came flesh and endured all the temptations we've ever had to face.

God has proven to me that he meant every word when he said he determines our steps (Prov. 16:9). Though we may of-ten feel lost and insignificant, he watches and guides as we place one dusty foot in front of the other.

None of his promises are to be taken lightly, swept be-neath rugs, or hidden out of sight. This life is an adventure comprised of glory and tribulations, and it is a beautiful revelation to know that he has determined each step down a beautifully broken road.

Yet I can't help but ponder brokenness and think about how much suffering is such a part of life, how we are conditioned to consider it destructive. When it comes to our wants and dreams for life, we don't understand why it can't be as easy as we dreamed; why must there be cracks and edges?

But the rock was struck and water flowed.

A mother's body breaks open to give birth to new life.

Jesus bled crimson on a wooden cross to save the world.

Maybe a broken heart isn't so bad.

Though there is no pain like that which is misunderstood, nor grief like that of the disenfranchised, Love promised it would still all be worth it. That brokenness and grief and flowing blood and water and even the somber taste of death meant undeniable, puritanical novelty. That if you at last could learn surrender, releasing clenched fists to old broken dreams, God could mend the tears to create tapestries of gold.

It's hard to let go of everything you've ever wanted. But it's harder to be out of the will of God.

Brokenness affirms the veracity that life was never supposed to be the fulfillment of our highlight reel of our perfect dreams and ideas, but a life spent loving and glorifing our Savior.

Only then can we joyously and honestly proclaim:

Hallelujah, you have saved me. So much better this way.

McKenna Vietti

Part I
Prothesis

McKenna Vietti

1

The Lure of Settling

*What is my future, that I
should be patient? (Job 6:11 BSB)*

Iᴛ's summer 2012. Acres of russet Southern California fields glow beneath sleepy sunlight that settles into sunset. I'm captivated, noting the way the light glows this summer evening, aware that another sensation burns within me. Even with eyes closed, I'm glimpsing something that light has recently exposed, a question that will patronize me for years to come. Something that should excite my sixteen-year-old self but instead finds its way into a corner of my brain where simplicity and peace should rest.

What do I do with my life?

Perhaps it wasn't the recent evening at a Calvary Chapel where they played a documentary of a lost little beach boy who became a pastor. It might have had nothing to do with the words of a woman who had moved to Uganda, adopted over ten children, started an organization, and then wrote a book about it. My mother reading biographies and stories of

Billy and Ruth Graham and even quotes from Mother Teresa shouldn't have stayed in my head for so long. But they did.

Maybe it wasn't any of those things alone.

Maybe it was *all* of them, God gently and quietly speaking into my heart in a way that has never happened before. Somehow, I recognize it. Even though it's a prodding completely unfamiliar, I've known that voice my entire life.

Words inside me don't rest until later when I'm sitting on my bed writing and they become nothing but muddles of thoughts that would implode into loss. I find myself doing it often; writing about feelings and thoughts that persist. As I reflect on recent entries of prose past, the same words explode all over the page like David beseeching the Lord in the Psalms. Words crying for direction, spattering ink like tears or perspiration; song lyrics and quotes that make better sense of my world than I can.

There aren't many moments in my life that I could define as revelation, but I believe that summer I turned sixteen was one of them.

In pale November light I can remember the living room of the house where we lived when I was three. A white cup with gold stars holds alabaster coffee—the only time my mom let me have it (comprised mostly of cream)—and she asks me, "Do you want to have Jesus into your heart?" I must have nodded yes. The next moment she was praying with me and I was repeating words I wouldn't understand for a lifetime to come, like love and grace and faith.

Words that I'm still learning to understand.

At twelve-years-old, I sat in the passenger's seat of my parents' gray Excursion while my dad drove following my mom as she biked up and over hills. Strength of faith in my family carried me until this age when I began questioning everything. My dad told me in love that doubt wasn't bad but could fortify my own beliefs. He told me to recognize the truth around me in creation that proclaimed proof of a Creator.

Childlike parts of me still run through the house when I shouldn't and laugh at inappropriate moments. But when it comes to my faith, it seems I need proof, even at twelve. My mind aches for evidence so my heart won't question anything ever again. I want to be sure. But how is anyone ever sure?

A different house and nearly eleven summers later, I sat on the balcony off my sister's room, anticipating an uncertain future as I read pages from a book written by a man who seemed to be a quarter-life crisis expert. Twenty-somethings are at a loss. Who of us has gone their entire life believing they would live up to something that only exists in childhood reverie? In time, we learn that life's not like that. Expectation of a life hopefully lived turns to disappointment. Like broken pottery, those childhood ambitions shatter and we're forced to recreate. The idea overwhelms us. Isn't it just easier to become someone else?

Thoughts of settling scared me more than never finding a purpose at all. There had to be a reason that trumped dissatisfaction, a word I would come to loathe. Nearly a college graduate with a loving family, the world a blank page before the story is written—it should have been enough. My life could be anything and I could be anyone.

My mind snaps repeatedly to that Southern California sunset; to that summer where Jesus took my hand and let me taste a bit of his sweet goodness that only left me running back for more. Through the use of other people, stories, and a stirring in my heart that proclaimed there was more to life than a nine-to-five, he whispered seeds into the muddiest parts of my heart, where beauty began to grow among thorns of uncertainty.

Dreams thrived.

Eventually that sixteenth summer passed. College approached and I knew my days to make a decision were narrowing. The ache to be more than ordinary was angst-filled and burdensome, yet exigent, and I knew I had to do more than simply exist.

It astounded me then, and it breaks my heart now, that so many people are failing to *live*. At some point, I started to realize the difference between living life and just simple survival. The fact that so many individuals seem to drift through life reminds me there is a great truth that either needs to be taught more or just emphatically recognized.

Is it because we are unsure of what to do? Are we scared of how to give up the urge to just settle? Do we not know how to live with purpose in a world where most, including ourselves, merely *survive*?

If any of you lacks wisdom, you should ask God, James says (Jas 1:5). But how often is asking God a last resort? Until disappointment has already sliced hope in half? Until our trembling hands can no longer take another of society's slapping rejections? Until we can no longer stand, so we hit our knees and curl into a position that begs consolation?

What do I do, God? Who am I supposed to be?

Uncertainty wears many faces. For some it walks in slowly, with prodding questions, then disappears while the doubts loiter in the mind long after. Others might see it and ignore, knowing it's probably a trap; something to be shrugged off before continuing with how they were.

But the outcome is the same. With all of us, uncertainty prompts questions and indecisiveness and the haunting *what if* that shrinks us back into the old routine of settling.

Numbly, we sit by the fireside, trying to warm our ideas and ambition to do something more; because we know that life, most definitely, is more.

We're just not sure of what to do.

And for years, the ache was there for me, but I didn't know what to do either.

2

Living Purposefully

"You knit me together. . ." (Psalm 139:13 NIV)

While college is painted as a colorful conjuring where you'll somehow find yourself, it doesn't always deliver. Questions dug holes in my heart as an eighteen-year-old. Somehow, the thousands of voices around me led me to believe that my purpose and career had to intertwine. We spend forty plus hours a week enslaved to our jobs. My profession would have to be a reflection of my dreams.

My first class on campus class was Introduction to Biology, and my first college friend was Leanna. We met after lecture, in the lab the first day of class, both too scared to go up to anyone else and ask if they wanted to be our lab partner. We ended up talking too much about competitive swimming and rock music and how neither of us was going to be a biologist anyway, so it was okay to show up late together after eating lunch at Trader Joe's instead of attending lecture. (Plot twist: we both ended up pursuing careers in healthcare).

In the middle of the semester, part of course credit was to attend a field trip to Oso Flaco Lake which, without telling Leanna, I decided to skip. I had driving anxiety and could hardly imagine trying to navigate to an unknown place.

"Are you going?" Leanna whispered after our professor made the announcement.

"No . . . I can't . . ."

She knew me all too well at this point. "You liar. You can too. Come on, I'll drive us. I'll buy you coffee."

A gray March afternoon later, we stood inside a Starbucks lobby waiting for flat whites, then climbed back inside her car. We drove down a rain-soaked highway until we reached our destination, where sun eventually broke through and light poured upon moist emerald leaves. Our professor and other students arrived, and we emerged from rain spattered cars, blazing a trail across soft clean soil.

Our professor led the group, stopping frequently to gesture at swaying trees and kneeling down to stroke purple leaves, simultaneously giving us the scientific name for everything as well as the name by which it was commonly known. We followed her across the dirt road as a covering of trees provided shade to our path. Between branches the sunlight glistened off her sunglasses as she moved from the plants growing from the Earth to the old pier that stopped just short of the lake. Our professor prompted us to be watching and listening as she effortlessly discussed the details of the life around us.

"I love how she does it." Leanna watched our leader as if she was our guide on an African safari.

"Does what?"

"I love how she just knows everything. Like, *all* of it."

It took me a moment, but then I understood what she meant.

It captivated us to watch someone so intricately understand the world around them. The professor understood not only the leaves rupturing with life, but the drenched flowers, the traces of wildlife, the bacteria of the waters. I stood speechless. Had I ever felt such certainty? What a gift to have such knowledge of any fragment of creation.

Biologists spend their lives trying to understand how organisms function and psychologists delve into the operations of human behavior. Once in a while, someone makes a discovery that blows the minds of everyone, but truthfully, we're just beginning to understand galaxies and oceans and the complexity of the human brain.

Years later, I realized that Jesus knows us even deeper than my professor knew the purple leaves.

Atoms, chromosomes, and every other fiber of intricacy are stitched into our being, as are a soul and a spirit; and he knows even those. He knows because he created it all. When we were woven together in the depths of the earth, not a part of us was hidden from him (Ps. 139:15). He wrote our days, ordained and breathed into existence (Job 14:5).

If who we are supposed to be is predestined for us, why do we worry? Is our concern mainly with ourselves and proving that we are somebody, or are we scared that we are going to spiral out of God's plan and become ironically ordinary?

It is written that he knows me, he knows you, he knows us. From the beginning, he knew us, and even now he knows far more than we know about ourselves. Over time, I slowly began to understand that purpose wasn't wrapped up in what I thought I *needed* to do or what others *expected* me to do; it had to be a reflection of who I *was*.

It wasn't in the *doing*, but in the *living*.

I lived under the impression that college would provide me the solution of discovering more about myself because a career—what this journey is mostly tied to—would define my purpose.

The college journey of trying to discover who I was lasted far too long. Tumultuous waves of decisions from changing majors to classes to wondering about graduate school exposed "you'll figure it out in college" as a dismaying lie. I graduated with no definite understanding of what I wanted to do, but did conclude three vital things:

1. I knew there was more.
2. I felt lost because I didn't know what I wanted.
3. I didn't know what I wanted because I didn't know who I was.

It took me a long time to pinpoint what it meant to live purposefully, but I recognized it when I saw it.

People who lived purposefully were zealous. This was not like the zeal of certain prominent figures whose names and faces graced the covers of magazines after they checked into a facility. Later, they would spend months or years of their lives speaking out against something it seemed they'd only recently discovered. These individuals were artists grafted into their perpetual darkness, glorifying the grim road upon which they walked and couldn't seem to turn right or left on to escape.

But there were other people too who *did* live purposefully and seemed to color the definition. They presented them-selves by *how they lived, not* by *what they were doing.* They were unafraid to travel across the borders in order to fulfill their life's calling. Rather than sitting beside the fireside allowing life to pass, they fearlessly sailed into the waves of life to preach and love radically as the Savior did. These were the people who lived completely and unashamedly surrendered to Christ. They seemed to be fully assured of their purpose and were living it out every single day.

I began to grow in the knowledge that there was more to life than sitting beside the firelight watching life pass. Living purposefully was no longer optional.

It became an obsession.

Maybe it was the coastal world I so fortuitously fell in love with—so much that I yearned to be a part of it. Although my roots clung to mountains, I wanted to live in this stunningly alluring world where waves washed away broken hearts and forgave my selfish desires. I loved the sherbet sunsets and pink sunrises and the smell of the sea. The silhouette of the palm trees against a midnight sky, the surreal allure of a balmy breeze as it hissed through the leaves, and the swoosh of the waves late into the night were supernaturally perfect—I could have wept at their beauty.

Through my job, church, and exploring the sandy beaches, I met people who piqued my interest and inspired me to soak up the wonders of this land. I watched as they lived in the surf, sun, and never-ending summer world. They existed physically near to me, but also hopelessly out of reach. I didn't know them, and they didn't really know me . . . not the way I wanted. Still, watching them live their lives influencing others influenced me to do the same.

I couldn't help but think to myself, *If this coastal town is this magical, what is the rest of the world like?*

I didn't have to take an office job or work eight hours a day or even have the weekends everyone else did. I didn't have to live out the tedious corporate work but could do a work I loved and reach other people at the same time. I wouldn't have to be like everyone else, and I didn't want to.

It became my mission to travel the borders of the world and touch the ragged edges with my fingertips in ways no one else had. While exploring this planet alone would be exciting, I knew I was destined to be more than a simple tourist. I knew that God had called me to do more than just travel.

Regardless of where I went—even if I stayed in this beautiful little beach town—I had to do *something* that was going to help heal the wounds that bled from the poorest of villages to the cracks of the metropolis.

In similar ways, the yearning to live differently—or live a life most others couldn't relate to—was therapeutically gratifying. For so many years of my young life I felt different, out of place, and pushed out of most circles. If I could do something that set me apart, I wouldn't feel so overlooked and different all the time. Or perhaps feeling set apart was a perfect foundation for that. Maybe I wasn't supposed to feel like everyone else because I wasn't meant to do what everyone else did.

In so many ways, the longing for purpose felt a lot like the longing for identity.

So my search began. There had to be something fulfilling enough that I could lay my head down every night convinced I was living life to the fullest.

It became more than evident that I *had* to live this way. When the end of my life came, either suddenly or slowly, I *had* to be ready with dirt beneath my fingernails because I planted seeds in life's soil while anticipating a holy rain. I wanted the handprints of children on my clothes as proof that I'd loved and tired eyes to prove my sleepless nights; mental exhaustion but spiritual fulfillment.

But complications followed. As we grow, we come to realize that our plans—no matter how pure—don't always promise to follow through. As I tried to grow roots in a world that I loved so much, everything abruptly changed. The roots were ripped from the shallow soil of the beach to a new world where everything looked and felt far different from what I had pictured for myself.

And I started to overthink. I learned that overthinking results in uncertainty, but I realized all my great questions could really be gathered into one:

How would my own great purpose be fulfilled?

3
The Setting Forth of a Thing

"He who began a good work in you
will carry it on to completion." (Phil. 1:6 NIV)

How do we know which dreams are from God? Do certain ones carry a holy essence, put into our hearts by our Creator who formed them as he formed us? Are they perfumed by his breath, unmistakable in our journey to discover ourselves?

Many of us make our plans while we are still young. Plans that are filled with anticipated hope, with blue papers on which schedules are written, new relationships are formed, the foundation upon which futures are built. As a young person, you are so enthralled with these plans that you never see the storm coming. Windows shatter. Something collapses. Like Ruth gathering up grain in an unknown field, we pick up the leftover bricks that once held our structure, trying to remember what it all looked like before and wondering if it is worth it to start over.

I wonder if dreams from God collapse over and over. Does he always use the storms to test our faith? Or does God use the crumbling to tell us to stop pouring our strength into something that isn't meant to be?

September 1, 2015, was the day my family and I traded in the coastal world for a Western, red dirt Northern California town.

I was nineteen. For four years, the beach, ocean, and the palm trees were my sanctuary; my roots clung to soft sand in place of earthy soil, and I didn't miss my original mountain home because I was someone different there. I liked who I was and the closeness of the dreams I was reaching for. Yet they still remained hopelessly out of reach, similar to how the waves repeatedly stretched toward the shore.

But in the red-dirt town, I didn't know what was waiting for any of us.

That early September morning, we woke before the sun and climbed into our cars packed with everything we owned. The engines purred down Highway 1 too quickly. I could hardly see the dark mass of ocean stretching to eternity on my left and I didn't know when I would see it again.

We arrived at the red-dirt town late that day. It was hot. And small. I felt parched from the moment we arrived, and I didn't know if it was from driving in the sun all day or because the sea roared hours away. Of course, the balmy breeze vanished and a still, warm whisper of the dry outdoors enveloped us in a suffocating welcome.

Our new home became a two-bedroom rental house named Valerie (the house had a name?) on the seamier side of town. It was small but workable. Our first night there, my family and I ate inside a locally owned Italian restaurant and talked about finally feeling settled again. *Landslide* played in the background and I scoffed at the accuracy.

I laid in my bed later that evening and tried to watch a movie that had comforted me countless times before; yet everything was disturbingly out of place. I stood up from my bed and stared out the window into the neighbor's backyard. The silhouette of a palm tree stood still and upright against a black sky.

I laughed.

Then I cried.

Leaving the world where my dreams were created meant my dreams were not coming where I was going. Rebuilding wasn't an option as much as reinventing. If my plans didn't align with God's, who was I supposed to be? What was I supposed to do? My world and all that was once a part of it was changed; no longer was I in a place where I felt the nearness of God. He had moved me, far from where I adored and where I had poured all of who I was, to a strange realm where I didn't recognize anything: not my dreams, or even myself.

I didn't give up on trying to understand purpose, even though time surged on and life suddenly began to look different in other areas. I started to feel different too. Maybe I wasn't born to be so extraordinary (although that felt a lot like settling and I wasn't sure why).

Through a difficult move from the coastal world that felt like home to a Western red-dirt town that felt so opposite, I started to wonder if I could be the same person in another place. I bounced from job to job, wondering why nothing ever felt right. I didn't want to settle but wanted to feel *settled*. I wanted a sense that I was finally where I should be.

Over the years, my questions seemed to be infinitely shallow. They were not questions of a twenty-something who'd been saved at three and had supposedly been growing and searching since sixteen; but questions of a Christian who had been living off milk too long. I thought more and more about identity and purpose and what it really was—if it looked the same for everyone. Is it something we are assigned at the beginning of life? Or is it simply a beautiful illustration of what some people choose to do? When we find our purpose, do we know? Is it a feeling? Do we choose it, or does it just happen?

Summers in the Western red-dirt town were beyond sweltering; they were stifling, and I concluded that I would never grow used to them.

It had been several years since the move. Countless times, I'd rearranged my books and my room and my life and still the questions lingered. I changed jobs, I changed my hair, I tried to change my perspective, but the uncertainty was as oppressive as the scorching California sun.

During one of these summers, several months after college graduation, I hunched over my desk absorbed in a dictionary of Greek and Hebrew words. I pause my eyes on that magical, mysterious word—the one that laid softly on the page as if it wasn't carrying the weight of a million questions.

I scanned the pages before me and came to a translation of the word that seemed to be more personal; maybe a word that's intended for our unique, individual use: *prothesis*. One of its usages is found in Romans: "To them who are then called according to his purpose [*prothesis*]" (8:28 KJV).

To *them*. Who are *called*. According to *his purpose*.

Moments passed and my immature perspective endeavored to wrap my mind around the fact that God called believers according to *his* purpose. God's purpose. For us to serve and love and glorify him.

I knew this, didn't I? I *knew* this because I'd done it. Through bi-weekly church attendance, mission trips, youth programs, summer camps, and Bible study, I'd done that and more since I could remember.

Somehow, I still missed something. I knew him and he knew me but maybe I took it all for granted. The realization of having a Savior who created me, knew me, and loved me hadn't made me fall to my knees recently, if ever.

I swallowed my doubt and pushed away the uncertainty that relentlessly followed me. I read more about *prothesis* and what it could mean for me and the rest of us searchers who had asked too many questions to be written off as simply curious doubters.

Prothesis: the setting forth of a thing.[1]

Setting forth of a thing. In this case—a more personal sense—it had to do with "them"—*our*—setting forth. It literally meant we have been destined for—set forth to

---

[1] William Smith, Smith's Bible Dictionary, (Barbour Publishing, 2012), s.v. "prothesis."

do—something. It is something that is set up to later be attained. Purpose describes fixed intention in doing something or the reason for which something is done or for which something (or someone) exists. It describes what one intends to accomplish or attain and suggests a settled determination: something that is going to happen.[2] " . . . and more than once is used as the word 'shewbread' in the Temple as exposed before God."

How and what does purpose have anything to do with the shewbread?

My lexicon referenced several passages in the Old Testament. In order to grasp the full context of *prothesis* and purpose, we need to understand the meaning of the shewbread.

In the Bible, shewbread is also known as the "bread of the Presence," or even "bread of the faces," and it's spoken of all throughout the Old Testament, specifically Exodus, 2 Chronicles, Leviticus, Deuteronomy, and 1 Samuel. Consider this passage from Exodus:

> Make a table of acacia wood—two cubits long, a cubit wide and a cubit and a half high. Overlay it with pure gold and make a gold molding around it. Also make around it a rim a handbreadth wide and put a gold molding on the rim. Make four gold rings for the table and fasten them to the four corners, where the four legs are. The rings are to be close to the rim to hold the poles used in carrying the table. Make the poles of acacia wood, overlay them with gold and carry the table with them. And make its plates and dishes of pure gold, as well as its pitchers and bowls for the pouring out of offerings. Put the bread of the Presence on this table to be before me *at all times.* (Exod. 25:23–30 NIV, emphasis mine)

---

[2] (Sermon Index-Purpose prothesis). Use the format of #1

Before the veil was torn, the holy place was a place in the temple where the priests could come into the presence of God. In this most sacred place sat a table, upon which sat the Bread of the Presence. Every Sabbath, twelve newly baked loaves (representing the twelve tribes of Israel) were placed upon the table in two rows and sprinkled with incense. There they would remain until the following Sabbath, at which point it would be replaced by twelve new ones. The incense was burned, and they were eaten by the priests in the holy place as a holy offering.[3]

Back in the Old Covenant era, the Lord commanded a beautifully specific ritual involving candlesticks, pitchers, bowls, and silverware that would come together and represent a holy offering to Yahweh. Sprinkled with frankincense, the smell of the bread intertwined with the incense and created a heavenly aroma that likely lingered long after the priests had left the holy place.

The loaves acknowledged that God was Israel's life source; they did not live on bread alone. Therefore, the table could never be without bread. Even after the priests had eaten the bread of the week before, given thanks, and acknowledged God as their life source, bread still had to be replaced, reminding the worshippers of their never-ending dependence on God.

It was beautifully specific, but what was the connection with purpose?

I had to reread the verses and several commentaries by scholars more gifted than I, but I reached this conclusion: When we come into the presence of the One who created us, we find our purpose.

---

[3] William Smith, Smith's Bible Dictionary, (Barbour Publishing, 2012), s.v. "prothesis."

Smith's Bible Dictionary puts it like this:

> The title "bread of the face" seems to indicate that bread through which God is seen, that is, with the participation of which the seeing of God is bound up, or through the participation of which man attains the sight of God whence it follows that we have not to think of bread merely as such as the means of nourishing the bodily life, but as spiritual food as a means of appropriating and retaining that life which consists in seeing the face of God.[4]

All the years of praying, wandering, and searching for purpose and meaning, I'd been diving into myself; an intricate system of DNA and soul and emotions. But when I surfaced, gasping for air, all I had was more questions.

We cannot try to make sense of who we are without looking at our Creator.

Our entire being proclaims him. Formed of dust but created in his image, our basic network consists of little proteins called laminins which, under close inspection, are literally in the shape of crosses. By him are things all held together (Col. 1:17). By him do we discover who we are.

I began whispering *prothesis* under my breath and thinking about the bread of the Presence and Jesus who is both the bread of life and living water. I know that when I come to him, I will never hunger or thirst. If my life is laid down before him, the hunger that comes with living a purposeful life and doing more than simply existing will vanish because I'm before my Maker; created in his image, living the life he's already ordained and set before me.

The wandering is gone.

---

[4] William Smith, Smith's Bible Dictionary, (Barbour Publishing, 2012), s.v. "prothesis."

The veil is torn.
The thirst to understand who we are is quenched.
Touching *him* puts us in touch with *who we are*.
By him, we can know and fully live our purpose.

4
The Burning Bush

We can know a powerful truth and still have no idea how to utilize its strength.

Prayer can be like this. Believers know how to pray. They know that it is, fundamentally, communing with God. But for many of us, prayer can be a last resort. Waves engulf, ship is sinking, and the crew throw themselves overboard in hopes God will deliver them through a big fish, whether they are swallowed or rescued. Either way, there's emancipation from the struggle. But only then does the thought of prayer come to the captain. Yet if he had just prayed at the beginning, the waves and wind could still likely come, but the ship and his crew would remain intact.

Prayer does that to a person (or in this case, a group of people). When we pray, setting aside our own doubts and desires, pouring out our concerns but still asking the Lord for his will, the storms may still arise, but we can remain strong.

Prayer is communing with God. We can't come away from speaking with the Creator of the universe and not be touched in some way.

We don't always believe prayer is going to change anything because what words would it take to change the will of God? What phrase, what chant can we use to change his mind?

The good news is we can't. We wouldn't want to change his will, his mind, or his ways to our own even if we could.

But why use it as a last resort? "All we can do is pray." If that is our response to any life struggle, then we *don't* know what prayer is or what it can do.

It's the same with purpose. We can have a basic understanding of what it is but have no idea how, when we fully grasp its meaning, it can change our lives.

Both prayer and purpose compel us to shift our gaze from ourselves and refocus our intentions back on God.

With each, we may begin by putting our own requests first. Both in our prayers and in our lives, it's easy to present what *we* desire to God. In prayer, we may (and usually do) have our specific requests we want God to answer. There's nothing wrong with presenting either to God, but with both prayer and purpose, we are required to go into his presence. We enter into the holy of holies when we pray. As we search for our purpose, we have to look to him in order to understand who we are.

When we do this, it shows us the differences between what we specifically request and what he wants for us and our lives.

We are realigned to his will when we pray and search for our purpose. God reminds us who we are; he brings us closer to him.

More than anything, our focus shifts from *us* to *him.*

Days after I discovered *prothesis* and how it relates to me, I sat in my room, books and Bibles littering the old oak desk, thinking about who else in the world had ever wondered about individual purpose and identity.

Flipping chapter by chapter through the Bible of my teen years, I remembered a baby who drifted down a river in a basket. He later grew into a man whose entire identity was wrapped into an Egyptian culture, ingrained in false beliefs and the idea that he belonged to a family contrary to the blood that ran through his veins.

> One day, after Moses had grown up, he went out to where his own people were and watched them at their hard labor. He saw an Egyptian beating a Hebrew, one of his own people. Looking this way and that and seeing no one, he killed the Egyptian and hid him in the sand. The next day he went out and saw two Hebrews fighting. He asked the one in the wrong, "Why are you hitting your fellow Hebrew?" The man said, "Who made you ruler and judge over us? Are you thinking of killing me as you killed the Egyptian?" Then Moses was afraid and thought, "What I did must have become known." (Exod. 2:11–14 NIV)

After he'd grown, something drew Moses to his own people, the Hebrews. It's quite possible—due to the murder of this Egyptian and having been nursed by his own mother—that Moses knew all along who he was. Or maybe he wanted to see the slave labor he was missing out on. Perhaps he thought he would be disgusted by the life he'd nearly been born into.

His response, however, wasn't one of disgust. As a man protective of his people, he murdered an Egyptian—one of the people who he'd probably come to consider as his own—for a man who really *was* his own. For a Hebrew.

Why would he do this? Moses was not a reckless, hot-tempered murderer, but a man slow in speech who would later become known for his humility.

Moses knew who his people were, and although murder is nothing to condone, he protected them at all costs—something God knew, saw, and would later use to bring his people from a life of slavery to the Promised Land.

After Pharaoh discovered that Moses had murdered a Hebrew, he tried to kill him. Moses fled Egypt to a place called Midian. There, he met Jethro, the high priest of Midian, who gave him a job tending his flocks. He also gave Zipporah—one of his daughters—to be Moses's wife.

One day, as Moses tended the flock of Jethro, he led them to the far side of the wilderness and came to a place called Horeb. An angel of the Lord appeared to Moses in flames of a fire within a bush. As Moses went over to the bush that, though engulfed in flames did not burn up, the Lord called to him. He commanded Moses to take off his sandals and said:

> "I have indeed seen the misery of my people in Egypt. I have heard them crying out because of their slave drivers, and I am concerned about their suffering. So I have come down to rescue them from the hand of the Egyptians and to bring them up out of that land into a good and spacious land, a land flowing with milk and honey . . . So now, go. I am sending you to Pharaoh to bring my people the Israelites out of Egypt." (Exod. 3:7–8, 10 NIV)

God defined Moses's purpose from the beginning. God spoke plainly and so explicitly to Moses. God clearly told Moses to go to Pharaoh and even *explained* to him *why* he wanted him to do what he called him to do. How did Moses respond?

- "'Who am I, that I should go to Pharaoh and bring the Israelites out of Egypt?'" (3:11)
- "'Suppose I go to the Israelites and say to them, "The God of your fathers has sent me to you," and they ask me, "What is his name?" What shall I tell them?'" (3:13)
- "'What if they do not believe me or listen to me?'" (4:1)
- "'I have never been eloquent'. . .'I am slow of speech and tongue.'" (4:10)
- "'Please send someone else.'" (4:13)

I don't know how long the conversation lasted, but I can almost hear Moses's voice coming up with every possible excuse he could muster to avoid doing what God told him to do. It's somewhat relatable.

- "Who am I? I'm no influencer!"
- "What am I even supposed to tell them when they ask who sent me?"
- "They're not going to believe me. What do I do then?"
- "I'm not a good speaker. I don't even want to speak, actually."
- "This isn't for me."
- "You should send someone else . . . please send someone else."

Again, God was incredibly straightforward. He gave Moses a purpose, a mission: deliver his people, the Hebrews. And he told him the first step in what he should do: talk to Pharaoh.

I read the words, trying to imagine the conversation that took place, and realized Moses's story is the epitome of *prothesis*.

Growing up in an Egyptian culture, raised as a prince, Moses knew what it meant to be a leader. He already had a great love for his people. He was given an incredible calling that would lead God's chosen nation to its own purposeful role in the greatest story in the world.

He was set forth to know both worlds. It was not a mistake for him to grow up knowing the luxury of Egypt. But in the face of a burning bush, Moses looked beyond himself and saw God the way the priests would later see him in the bread.

Beyond his role of a prince or a Hebrew in a foreign land, Moses fulfilled his calling when he saw the Lord and obeyed.

Not all of us are chosen to lead nations in this modern world.

Some believers today are given notoriety that allows them to reach the masses through traveling, speaking, and crusades. These figures are the people who inspired me from the beginning, causing me to believe they believed in something powerfully life-changing.

They dedicated their lives to proclaiming the truth.

But few of us are truly called to that, and I'm not certain how many of them set out with the intention of reaching the masses. Much of it comes from simple obedience and faith. It comes from asking God what he wants us to do and then stepping out, trusting God do his work.

If I heard God's voice in my ear, telling me exactly which steps to take, would I still doubt and question? Would I ask how would it come to pass? Would I strain for more information and long to see the entire journey before me?

We can't fool ourselves. I would want to see the entire tapestry. I can't ridicule Moses for asking God questions when I have the Bible—the Guidebook to this overwhelming life—accessible to me. It brims with instructions on what I am called to do as a believer and what the Lord expects of me if I'm to truly serve him with my life.

That is the mystery of it all. If we knew the power we *really* had because of the Holy Spirit, if we *really* knew all the answers to life's greatest questions—including questions of identity and purpose—could be found in God's Word, I doubt we would ever struggle with uncertainty of *prothesis* ever again. It is not hidden in the pages or the bread. Our personal purpose is wrapped into our calling as believers.

A verse I have kept close to me since the uncertainty began is found in the book of Jeremiah. It's one that most of us know and often is taken out of context: "'For I know the plans I have for you,' declares the Lord, 'plans to prosper you, and not to harm you, plans to give you hope and a future'" (29:11 NIV).

It occurred to me recently that God says he has *plans* for us. Not a *purpose* but plans. I still whisper *prothesis* under my breath because I know that only in the face of God do I discover who I am, but what is this about plans? Is that the same as purpose?

It's no surprise that the verses that come after this one are, "'Then you will call upon me and come and pray to me, and I will listen to you. You will seek me and find me when

you seek me with all your heart. I will be found by you'"
(29:12-14 NIV). We question purpose and plans and go to God
in the uncertainty, and he promises that we will find him. He
doesn't promise we will find our purpose or a blueprint for
life plans but *him*.

What does that really tell us?

It's only confirmation that our plans, purpose, and calling
are found in him and him alone. When we realize that powerful truth, when we embrace our identity in him and know
our purpose and calling is the essence of who he is, we will
undoubtedly find incredible purpose living a life that only he
could plan for us.

McKenna Vietti

Part II
Identity

McKenna Vietti

5

Who We Are

Four years had passed since moving to the hot Northern California town.

One late summer evening, I sat in the backyard on the edge of the pool, feet dangling in the glass blue water, head tilted upward and staring at the stars dancing between the branches. I closed my eyes, thinking of the opportunity that stretched before me.

Over the summer, the pastor of my church asked if would pray about becoming a teacher for a small private school that was part of the church's ministry. I toppled between the idea of a stable teaching career and falling into that lure of settling, but it was far too good of an opportunity. As soon as I told my pastor yes, he and half the members of my church congratulated me on my decision, assuring me that I would make a fabulous teacher. Pride was my initial response, but later my heart sank to murky, mysterious depths.

I couldn't imagine becoming a teacher, and not because I considered it devastatingly ordinary. The distance from that and what I wanted for my life was immeasurable.

Following my decision, I received texts, phone calls, and frequent stops on my way out of church from parents asking what supplies and project materials I would need for the upcoming year. Grandparents offered to volunteer. Another well-meaning friend offered to hold a reading group for my class because she knew one of my students would need some additional help with comprehension.

Most of my responses came from forced smiles and confidence. I was being asked to conduct class projects and reading groups, yet I didn't even know what it meant to write lesson plans.

The stars shone, a breeze blew, my dog beside me looked up as a truck drove over gravel in the alley. I opened my eyes and glanced back toward the house from where light poured and my siblings' happy voices beckoned me to come back.

Not yet. Waves surged in my heart—emotions that felt like anger, fear, and regret, and I wasn't sure why. My mind swam in a fog and my thoughts grew unclear. Days before, I laid on my bed with tears streaming down my face, begging that God would somehow take this burden from me.

Why do I always feel so uncertain? What am I putting before you, Lord?

A still, calm voice whispers back: *Yourself.*

A year flew by. In the midst of student names and faces, I came to see each one as a precious soul that God entrusted to my trembling hands to hold. I prayed I wouldn't fail these teenagers, so young in their walk with God. I prayed that they would find Jesus despite my painfully inadequate attempts. I know there was at least one I didn't fail. He was the boy who everyone shrugged off, made fun of, thought of as odd because he was a little different (or a lot different).

Joey started the year off as an atheist. His hand shot up multiple times each morning during our devotions. I was going through the Gospel of Mark, trying to introduce Jesus to these teenagers who didn't know him otherwise. Joey never failed to have a question—or contradiction—for nearly everything I said.

He was smart. He thought critically, and I often didn't know how to answer him.

"You tell us to search God's Word for ourselves," he scoffed at me one day, sitting back in his seat and making sure his classmates could hear him (likely so he could get a good laugh at the end). "And yet you just said we're to be like a little kid and believe. How does that make sense?"

I can hardly remember my response. I do remember promising myself that once the year ended, I would never waste my time trying to teach or get through to incorrigible youth ever again.

Our morning devotions continued. We finished our passage for the day, and I told my students to close their Bibles and begin their morning work. Everyone did as they were told . . . except Joey. About an hour later, I looked up from my desk to see his Bible was still open to the book of Mark. His head rested in both of his hands, and he was completely engrossed.

I almost felt bad for telling him to close his Bible and work on his algebra. But that would be the first of many times I caught him reading Scripture instead of doing his assignments.

Weeks later, I had to send a message to Joey's mom and let her know he was failing English. The next day, he pulled me aside and asked if there was a way he could earn extra credit, since he knew I was probably not going to reassign the quizzes and assignments he had failed.

In the midst of my anger and doubt, an opportunity had seemed to present itself. "Alright," I said. "Let me put something together, and you can take it or leave it." I went back to my desk and found several parables from the Gospels. I printed them out and waited until lunch to present the assignment to him. "You have three weeks to study these, create a presentation, and then teach the class what you think they mean," I told him. As I laid out the guidelines, I could see him studying my printed directions. Then he looked me in the eye and simply nodded.

Joey did not disappoint. The morning of his presentation, he stood dignified at the head of the room and taught the same peers who never missed an opportunity to make fun of him. To my surprise, he didn't just pick one parable to interpret but all three.

Several years later, his mom posted a video of him on Facebook leading the entire school in morning devotions—praying, delivering a message, and calling others to live for Jesus—as he had made the choice some time ago.

When my year of teaching had finished, I recalled the mornings spent praying at the steering wheel in my car as I drove that short commute to the school. There were days when my stomach churned and I wondered how in the world I was going to make it another day responding instead of reacting, watering souls, living out God's truths, and not shoving it down their throats.

I think back on the days during lunch hour where I locked my classroom door, unplugged the phone, and maybe even turned off my own device just so my mind would have a moment to rest. There were the students that pushed every last button regardless of detention notes or hallway prayers. Moments throughout the day, I wanted to clobber walls but resorted to sobbing in bathroom stalls. There were days I came home and could do nothing more but sit on my bed and stare at my wall as the sun sank into the night, thinking about how I would have to wake up too early to do it all over again.

I told my mom nothing in the world could make me go back to teaching again, even if it meant I could live in my dream home on a remote island, hundreds of miles away from the school and a job I never wanted and didn't ask for.

But would I do it again to help a lost soul find home?

This, beloved, I can hear my Father say, *is what you were created for.*

Life and joy and purpose were not wrapped up in teaching or a career, nor were they ever. I'd expected purposeful living to be attached to the adrenaline rush of watching cities fall on their knees in repentance, witnessing tears fall with joy, seeing hopeful hearts change stubborn minds. I wanted to be part of that revelation where I could physically see the spiritual things happen. Not the boring stuff. Not the mundane waking up at sunrise to ponder the long day ahead and plant small seeds in small places while somehow living out grace stuff.

But it's about the mundane, isn't it? Isn't it about not just reaching, but *touching* the souls, even if it's only one after a dry, miserable year? Or five years? Or ten years?

One year of teaching was enough for me—but I did discover the answer to that question.

Somehow, at a tiny school, in a career I most definitely didn't ask for or even want, *prothesis* still managed to weave its way into my life. Regardless of how much I loved (or didn't love) my work and my life, and despite the fact that my identity turned into something I never wanted to become . . . I could still serve God. My attitude probably wasn't the best most days; but he worked through me, in spite of me.

The Lord set forth a plan for a wanderlust driven, ocean-bound, hopeless adventurer to take on the task of caring for the souls of ten teenagers. At the time, all I could see was how pathetic my life had become. Who could find joy in a small school full of teenagers who didn't appreciate someone who was giving up so many dreams to come to work and serve them? They had little respect for me, cheated on assignments, and cursed on their lunch break seconds after I prayed over them.

Only God knew what the years to come would bring. Despite all our shortcomings, my students and I stay in touch, even today. I've received messages from some of them and keep in contact with their parents. They remind me about that year and what it meant to them. I have seen others choose to give their lives to the Lord, serving in the church and going on mission trips and telling their peers about their God.

It's quite obvious now that serving in a small school for only one year could be just as fruitful as traveling the world.

Even in the parched mundane land, *who* we were created to be defines *what* we were created to do. Meaning, in order to understand *what* we were meant to do, we must first understand—and accept—*who* we were created to be.

6

Identity Crisis

We are woven into Adam and Eve's story in Genesis: who we came from, where we began, and how we were supposed to live.

In a few short verses, beauty is tarnished. Sin entered the world and perfection vanished. Roses grew thorns. Animals became vicious. Sickness invaded and death was inevitable. How often did Adam and Eve think about how the Garden was before sin entered? Certainly, they missed it. Over the thousands of years of humankind, they were probably the ones who thought the most about how life was not supposed to be this way.

It is what it is now, so what do we make of it? We were born into sin. But what does that mean for us? Who were we *really* created to be?

It can be easy to fall into an identity crisis when we start thinking too much about these questions. Digging into God's

Word has the power to open eyes and reveal a beautiful understanding: he *did* create us with incredible intent and purpose. We are destined to "become somebody" (as my teenage self may have put it). We were created to do more than settle for the ordinary, and far more than just exist. When we understand these truths and fully believe them, we will find ourselves living up to that calling.

But first, let's determine who we are *not*. We are not:

- An IQ
- Bad grades
- Good grades
- A number on the scale
- A career
- A relationship
- An Enneagram number
- A Myers-Briggs type
- An ethnicity
- A hobby (or many)
- A success
- A failure

It's true that those things can be determined. They can make us feel differently. They can be a source of our joy or heartache. They can, perhaps, even make other people like us more (or less).

Many of us believe the lie that all these aspects of ourselves (our appearance, successes, failures, the way we respond to things, etc.) determine who we are. Are they bad? Not necessarily. Do they define who we are? With all the assurance I can muster: *absolutely not.*

They are nothing more than embellishments. They set us apart a little, but who we truly are—who we were created to be—goes much deeper and is richer and more vibrant than any of those things.

In Psalm 139, the psalmist talks about how deeply and fully known we are by God. To be known doesn't mean God knows only *about* us. Of course, he does know about us. I know where Taylor Swift was born, how many homes she owns, how many men she's dated, and possibly which songs are about which men—but do I *know* her? No. Because knowing someone is so much more than just knowing *about* them.

The psalmist states that our thoughts are known by God. Our comings and goings are known by God. Our ways are known by God. He knows our words before they are even on our tongue. We can magnify the smallest detail, the most intricate of cells, and God is already there.

Even more, *he is always there.* He didn't create our inmost being in the beginning and then allow us to wade uncertainly through life. Whether we can admit to it or not, we all change dramatically over the years. I know I have. Over the past twenty-something years, it seems as if I've morphed into a completely different person. From careers to relationships to ideas to character growths and developments, God has held my hand every step of the way.

Through each change, heartbreak, breakdown, joy, and progression, God remained with me. I can't escape his presence. I can't run from his Spirit. From the depths of the earth to the far side of the sea, he is with me, just as he is with you.

For Someone who knows us so well, how could our outer appearance, achievements, career, or anything else define us to him? If your sister cuts her hair, does that change who she is? If your best friend changes careers, does he become a better person?

The bottom line is this: we cannot base our value on anything we do or look like but on *who we are in Christ*.

There's an invisible string tying us to God. We were made in his image, so when we look to him, we can see who we were created to be. Our value does not come from us; it comes from him and is found in him. We need to do more than just know that or memorize it; we must embrace it, hold it, and understand what a glorious, freeing truth it is. To do this, we must be continually spending time with him, understanding his heart, and his will for our lives.

Who we are in Christ and who we *feel* like we are are often two very different things. Many of us decide to believe what feels right rather than what is true because *feelings sometimes feel stronger than truth*. This is why so many of us—myself included—try to do things on our own. We've invested in something other than Christ.

Other people sometimes go a different direction. Maybe they give up because they believe they don't possess anything worthy or they themselves are not worthy. They feel that they as people have no worth outside of achievements or appearances. There was a time in my life (and even now at times) I felt this way. I invested a great deal into my image, how I carried myself, and how people thought of me.

Once I was asked to speak at a small church service one evening. Although public speaking was (and continues to be) one of my greatest fears, I believed I had done enough public speaking in my life that I didn't really need to prepare. It was a small church service, after all, and I could wing it for just one evening, right?

I quickly learned that winging it shouldn't be a consideration for anything—especially public speaking.

The evening did not go as planned. I botched my entire presentation and drove home in a pathetic, self-pitiful silence, convinced I was an utter failure. I had a sort of mental breakdown and believed I couldn't do anything right.

Talk about identity crisis.

I share this story to dramatically (or comically) emphasize the point that who we truly are and how we feel are two very different realities. Whether we are basing our self-worth on achievements, failures (public speaking escapades included), outside opinions, or something else, *that is not who we are.* We can spend ridiculous amounts of time and energy building our personal palaces and trying to prove we are someone by what we are doing—but that, too, is a falsity.

The idea that we have no identity, that we are not unique, special, or worthy is rooted in lies.

Sometimes I marvel at the ever-growing and popular modern catch phrases like self-worth, self-care, self-help, among others. I don't have to spell out what they all have in common. Self, that four letter word that looks so small and innocent, may be the glorified suicide of my generation.

I'm not denying the fact that self-care is important. We need to cultivate our own mental health. There's nothing wrong with taking a few selfies every now and then—or fifty if your curls are popping. I can admit that I've probably overemphasized the importance of self-care and taken far too many selfies when golden hour hit.

But I also know what happens when these habits become the norm. When we look at ourselves too often, we begin thinking too much about ourselves . . . and this is where it gets complicated. If we constantly focus on ourselves—be it our achievements, careers, relationships—it is incredibly easy to lose sight of Christ.

That is why it is so important to look to him and who he says we are.

And honestly, who is that? What does that look like? Who are we in him? What is it that we can embrace and consume ourselves with so tightly that everything else falls away?

7
The Mission

"You also, like living stones, are being built into
a spiritual house to be a holy priesthood, offering
spiritual sacrifices acceptable to God through
Jesus Christ." (1 Peter 2:5 NIV)

There is a poem by Nikita Gill called *Space Theories* that introduces the reader to another world. It describes this land somewhere across the universe where forests float on water and whales dance across the sky and the people are given a choice to love or live forever.[5]

I don't imagine a universe so much like this, where one has to choose between temporary love or eternal life (because I know in heaven we'll have both). If I'm imagining another universe, or any other place besides heaven, my imagination runs wild with ridiculously beautiful worlds.

While Tolkien gave us the Shire and C.S. Lewis introduced us to Narnia, I always go back to the sea. Maybe

---

[5] Gill, Nikita. "*Space Theories.*"

instead of gravel streets, there are Venetian waterways. The weather isn't always seventy-four degrees and sunny; there are warm rainstorms, gardens filled with sea turtles, and kite festivals. The sand appears gold. The people are kind, and there isn't a great need for criminal justice.

Somehow, life is simpler. I tend to imagine a world before social media and complex technology and convoluted government administrations. Instead, there is a king who settles matters, orchestrates solutions, and facilitates whatever needs to be done. Whether the issue is great or small, the king is both good and willing. He is busy, but he cares for each need, and he is never too busy to assist the people with any plight.

Imagine yourself in this world. Say that you are one among the millions of villagers. One day, something happens in your world, and it entices you to see this king; the only one who can solve matters. Perhaps a family member is ill. There's a leak in your roof. Or maybe there's an especially pesky neighbor and you need advice on how to handle circumstances.

There are steps you can take—take your ill relative to the local physician; repair the leak yourself; compromise with the neighbor—but the only one who can truly help you, is the king because he is the one who assesses the problem and ensures a solution.

Of course, there are other villagers who need help. The wait could be miles long. Especially if the others have bigger problems and you just have a leaky roof. Your problems, it seems, are far less important. The woman with the sick child, the man dying from bone cancer . . . certainly this king would help them first before he bothers to see you.

Still, you decide to make the journey. You depart your leaky-roofed home complete with sick family and annoying neighbors, and paddle your way to the glittering palace resting on the gold beach. When you arrive, the palace doors open, and you are escorted into the throne room.

Surprise catches you, for there are no lines.

No attendant ushers you to leave your name and number so they can call you back.

Not even a veil of separation.

You only see the King, sitting on his throne in all his glory, smiling at you with open arms. He's more than ready and willing to hear about the troubles of your home and heart. Not only does he invite you into his glittering palace on the cliffs of the sea, but he desires you to stay longer than you planned.

You walk toward him. He grasps your hands and pulls you into an embrace that makes you realize how small you and your troubles really are—not because you're insignificant, but because he is so significant.

How? you ask. *How could you be sitting there, just waiting to hear about me and my so-called life?*

He smiles at you, squeezing your hands, ensuring you how overjoyed he is just to have you with him.

Simple, he responds. *You believed I would meet you here.*

I often forget I have unlimited access to the God of the universe simply because I am a believer. Peter tells us that all believers are priests (1 Pet. 2:9). This means we have a special privilege: God bends his ear to us. Not only that, but as a priest, we have opportunities for ministry.

That is the overall mission of the church. We are called to minister to others through worship and service. But what does that look like?

> "And it was he who gave some to be apostles, some to be prophets, some to be evangelists, and some to be pastors and teachers, to equip the saints for works of ministry, and to build up the body of Christ, until we all reach unity in the faith and in the knowledge of the Son of God, as we mature to the full measure of the stature of Christ." (Ephesians 4:11–13 BSB)

Consider this: the God of the universe, the One who created galaxies, music, oceans, chromosomes, neurons, and emotions, would choose the broken people of the world to tell other broken people about himself. I'm (obviously) not God; but I often think about how much I would probably do differently if I were.

Why would he choose *us*? Why would he use people who offend, sin, and forget to prepare for presentations to speak to the lost children of the world? Isn't he afraid we're going to make irreparable mistakes? Yet God gave some to be apostles, prophets, evangelists, pastors, and teachers. These are not easy roles to be taken lightly.

I read once that ministry life (like teaching) requires a soft heart and thick skin. It's not a job to cast aside as if it were a simple nine-to-five. It requires harvesting, planting, and reaping, over and over again. Those who are called to ministry have their thoughts and daily lives consumed with it, probably more than any of us realize.

A pastor friend of mine uses simple conversations to tell the gospel to the Starbucks barista or the airline pilot. He is someone I would imagine Paul is referring to in Ephesians. My friend is not famous for preaching but he embodies an evangelist. When I accompanied him and his wife and another couple on a mission trip to Honduras years ago, I came to understand what it really looked like to evangelize.

We headed back to our quarters one evening, walking the moist dirt road back to our rooms, when a homeless man stopped us. My friend began walking with him in the opposite direction we were heading and his wife laughed. "We may as well get comfortable," she said. "We'll be here a while." We joined arms and walked to the nearby gelato shop.

Up until then, I'd always envisioned evangelism as people standing on soap boxes in the middle of a town square. Regardless of where he was or what he was doing, my dear friend always seemed to fit Jesus into the conversation.

Some believers are born evangelists.

I have another friend who was born to be a teacher and has the privilege of teaching at a Christian school. Her voice, personality, and being embodies what most would imagine when they picture an elementary school teacher; beyond that, though, her teaching is influenced by the Spirit who lives within her.

What about the rest of us? What about a timid public speaker who is miserable when teaching? Does that mean we can't teach or evangelize? Does it mean we don't have a specific role like the other "chosen ones?" I think we know the answer to that would be a resounding no.

Does that mean there are other roles or callings at which we might be better? Are there certain jobs the Lord has specifically called us to?

God mentions roles besides those of teachers, evangelists, and pastors. "We are therefore Christ's ambassadors, as though God were making his appeal through us. We implore you on Christ's behalf: be reconciled to God" (2 Cor. 5:20 NIV).

Let's think back on the mission of the church. We know that the gospel is spread and the kingdom advanced most rapidly through the active church (Christians). Now, the Christian is not just an individual who is saved but someone who has been born into the family of God (identity) and baptized into the body of Christ (purpose).

Every Christian, therefore, needs to be an active member of Christ's body. This is what is meant by *ambassador*.

An ambassador represents someone or something. As Christians, we represent Christ to a broken and fallen world.

This can be through virtually anything.

Let's break it down into two simple truths: 1) as believers, we have unlimited access to God and 2) through this access, we can reach a lost world.

This means serving the suffering (mentally, physically, spiritually, emotionally). It means building up one another.

As ambassadors, we are given a huge responsibility; God entrusts us with souls, not only to care for them, but to act as personal witnesses as believers in Jesus Christ. Not only do we have unlimited access to God, but we are literally called on this special mission to love and worship. God called some to be evangelists, pastors, teachers, missionaries; others are called to serve on behalf of the *entire* people of God.

How can we *not* take this lightly? We have a great responsibility as those who have accepted Christ as our Savior.

Before we go deeper, I want to emphasize that we should not become overwhelmed or consumed with works. Scripture declares countless times that the perfect blood of Jesus Christ saves us—nothing else.

We cannot work our way to heaven and we shouldn't even try. It is by the grace of God and the blood of his Son Jesus that any of us can get there.

If you are struggling to find purpose, wondering who you are or what you are supposed to do with your life, this is your answer.

Do you want purpose? Do you want to change the world in a radical way? *Go out* into all the world. Tell them about the Savior who died for you and grafted you into his holy family. Care for the one or two or thirty souls he has entrusted to you, and don't you dare tell me he hasn't. If you are a daughter, sister, son, grandfather, neighbor, student, nurse, engineer, receptionist, or mechanic, there are souls around you and you are called.

You are more than a villager paddling down a watery road, searching for a way to heal the sickness and bear the burden of a leaky roof and an unruly neighbor. Some days may look like dusty mundane drudgery that holds burdens too difficult to bear. But one day you will sit in heavenly glory, for you are a priest. No longer a slave, but a child and an heir (Gal. 4:7). One day, after death has been conquered and we are allowed our crowns of glory, we will inherit the Kingdom of God; the sparkling spiritual realm we can now only imagine.

What enters the mind when you picture a priest, ambassador, or saint? They are beautiful, glorious words for a people destined to be glorious. How can we still feel lost and purposeless when we know we were meant for glorious royalty?

Like the shewbread, you are set apart. You have been destined for an earthly mission that no one else can fulfill. Because you are an ambassador, you have meaning. You have been set forth to represent Christ in however many opportunities he offers you. You have a divine purpose. Believe me when I say it's not at all what you imagined.

It's far better.

8

Chasing the Road to Damascus

*"For we are God's workmanship, created in Christ Jesus
to do good works, which God prepared in advance
for us to do." (Ephesians 2:10 BSB)*

In January, during that year of teaching, I took a week off
from my position to travel with two missions-minded couples
to a missionary conference in Murietta. Nothing could have
been more inspiring than listening to the stories of missionaries from all over the world as they told of their lives
abroad.

The flight home, I stared out the window of the
Southwest Airlines plane, onto the jagged snowy peaks of
Sacramento. All I wanted was to return to normal life. I was
disturbed in a totally new way. While I had felt uplifted and
inspired, knowing that the only way we can truly change the
world was by sharing the love of Jesus to mankind who

cannot save themselves, I was frightened. I couldn't be sure if I was being called into this life of total abandon, leaving my family and friends and beloved Rottweiler to go to a desolate land where the name of Jesus was rarely spoken, or to stay in the town I was growing to be a part of. If I didn't go, what would I be missing out on? How many souls were waiting across the sea for someone to bind up the brokenhearted and whisper hope into the forlorn places?

If I hadn't said yes to teaching and spent that year with my ten teenagers, I would have been more comfortable. My twenty-third year would have consisted of better rest and discovering what I wanted for my life. I might have applied to grad school or gotten a better job that paid more money so I could finally wander the streets of Turin or go back to Honduras.

But if I hadn't been at that school . . . who would have? Would anyone have stepped up?

I used to be so scared of growing comfortable.

Now I was scared of actually being obedient.

On the last evening of the conference, one missionary shared something that wouldn't minister to me until months later. I carefully wrote it down in my notes for future reference:

When the church is focused on its mission of making disciples, the disciples go out and change the world.

The morning we left the Murietta campus, I walked from my dorm to the main hall to meet my friends for breakfast. I watched the bubbling hot springs meet chilly January air. Steam formed, then quickly dissipated into nothing.

I wondered about how much we want to save the world, or at least change it. How much less I wondered about the millions of souls inside. And my heart spoke a truth I didn't want to face: the glory of men often feels more appealing than the glory of God. Not because the glory of men is irresistible—it's just quicker and easier and gratifies my fleshly desires. But truthfully, it's nothing more than steam from the hot springs. It comes and goes. People forget. What was stunning for a moment doesn't last forever, and neither does the recognition.

I stood frozen in the mid-winter wind and continued to feel unsettled. In the midst of hundreds of missionaries who had obediently answered the call, I was still asking God who I'm supposed to be.

In the race of life—whether it's about survival or about living in a way that's more than just existing—the focus falls unequivocally on ourselves. Is most of our time on Earth spent living up to our calling or trying to find it?

How do I live gloriously? I stared across the campus at the swaying palm trees and a sparkling fountain. A wind blew up, and the cold water gently sprayed across my face. What more is earthly glory than droplets of water that sparkle for a moment but then evaporate in the sun and are just as forgotten? With each session I attended, my convictions grew stronger: what could be a more glorious purpose than becoming a missionary?

In time, a new truth would be revealed in ways that would shatter me: it wasn't about what I was *doing*, it was about how I was *living*.

It wasn't about me; it was about him.

And maybe it was a revelation that I had known for a long time but just hadn't accepted. At last, I was finally bringing my vulnerable, delicate hopes and dreams for my life to my Father, but they were nothing new to him. My ideas may have been outlandish, but couldn't God use them too? He starts the work in us from the beginning (Phil. 1:6), yet we try to change the course. These ponderings brought me back to the question of personality, individuality, and uniqueness; about a defined calling; and even more so, about our identity in Christ.

Was there an answer to all this?

I couldn't always see it, but the truth stood out like snow on a mountaintop. How could God name each star and not distinguish each of his children? The truth of individuality and purpose shines iridescently in a plastic world. It looks different for everyone *because it is*. It reveals our identity. It reveals our calling. We become saturated in a river that is deeper than "the one reason we are born."

A powerful example of *prothesis* happened to one of the most influential Christian leaders in history.

In the book of Acts, we read about a man named Saul who was notorious for persecuting Christians. He was passionate about opposing the name of Jesus of Nazareth and destroying the acts of the apostles. Saul was convinced that it was necessary to do everything he could to oppose the name and to persecute the people who loved and served him. Saul locked up saints in prison and put them to death. He traveled from synagogue to synagogue, punishing and killing those who followed Christ. He was enraged at them; so much so that he even pursued them to foreign cities.

With the authority and commission of the chief priests, Saul traveled to the city of Damascus, unknowingly on his last journey in opposition to Jesus. During his journey, he saw a light from heaven, which he described as "'brighter than the sun, blazing around me and my companions'" (Acts 26:13 NIV). Saul and his companions fell to the ground, and he heard a voice speak to him.

"'Saul,' the voice asked. 'Saul, why do you persecute me? It is hard for you to kick against the goads'" (v.14). The voice (the Lord) was telling Saul he couldn't keep resisting the pleadings of the Holy Spirit.

In response, Saul cried out, "'Who are you, Lord?'" (v. 15).

"'I am Jesus, whom you are persecuting,' the Lord replied. 'Now get up and stand on your feet'" (v.15–16).

The Lord went on to tell Saul that he had appeared to him that day to appoint him as a servant and a witness of what he has just seen, and what he was going to see. Everything Saul had done, and everything he was, was getting turned around. No longer was he to stamp out the name of Jesus; instead, his new mission was to tell people that the Lord had appeared to him, and he was to go to them and teach them what he knew.

There was the Saul before the road to Damascus. He was the man who murdered and planned murders and hated the name of Jesus. Prior to Damascus, Saul's purpose was to kill those who loved and followed Jesus and shared his truth. I doubt Saul thought of much else. I envision him staying up most nights, sitting beneath the dark sky, face glowing in the evening moonlight, burning with a passion to stamp out the name of Jesus. As a Pharisee in Jerusalem, Saul had probably heard of this radical rabbi. I even wonder if he went to Golgotha to watch the crucifixion of the miracle-working Carpenter from Nazareth.

When darkness covered the land at the moment Jesus died, the veil was torn in two, and the earth shook. Even with claims of the stone being rolled away with no body laying inside, Saul continued on the road of persecuting Christians until he was on the one to Damascus.

Then everything changed. Though he began the journey breathing out murderous threats to destroy the synagogues proclaiming the name of Jesus, he encountered a light and a voice from heaven that blinded him for three days. Acts 9:6 says the Lord told Saul to go into the city, blind as he was, and there he would be told what to do next.

Meanwhile, God had already made plans for someone to meet Saul in Damascus. While Saul continued trudging down the road, blinded and most likely shocked by what had just occurred, God was already working in the life of another man who would be instrumental in Saul's life purpose.

His name was Ananias. Around the same time Saul was traveling that metamorphic road, the Lord was calling to this man in a vision:

"'Go to the house of Judas on Straight Street and ask for a man from Tarsus named Saul, for he is praying . . . he has seen a man named Ananias come and place his hands and restore his sight'" (Acts 9:11–12 NIV).

Apparently, Ananias knew exactly which Saul the Lord was referring to. "'Lord,'" he said. 'I have heard many reports about this man and all the harm he has done to your saints in Jerusalem . . . he has come here . . . to arrest all who call on your name!'" (v.13–14).

These men who had such clear instructions from God responded with questions and statements, as if they need to fill God in on what's really going on.

The Lord prompted Anaias: "'Go! This man is my chosen instrument to proclaim my name to the Gentiles and their kings and the people of Israel . . . he must suffer for my name'" (v.15–16).

Maybe the fact that he knew Saul was going to suffer gave him the stimulus to follow through. Or maybe he was simply submitting to God. Whatever the reason, Ananias obeyed and went to the house where God had commanded him to go. He placed his hands on Saul and uttered a prayer:

> "'Brother Saul, the Lord—Jesus, who appeared to you on the road as you were coming here—has sent me so that you may see again and be filled with the Holy Spirit.' Immediately, something like scales fell from Saul's eyes, and he could see again. He got up and was baptized, and after taking some food, he regained his strength." (Acts 9:17–19 NIV)

From that moment on, Saul became the apostle who would go on to write letters that would form a sizable percentage of the New Testament. He would indeed suffer for the name of the Lord, in foreign lands, in prison cells, and in torture. He went from destroying the name of Jesus to proclaiming it.

Like Moses, Paul discovered his purpose when he looked to God. *Prothesis. The shewbread.* Only when we look to God do we find ourselves.

I wonder if, like Saul, we too need to be blinded to see our purpose. Maybe we need some things to be taken away from us—maybe our sight, maybe a job—in order to understand who we are *not*. What if, instead of wandering the road to Damascus, we search long and hard after it? We would become ambassadors on an earthly mission for Christ, passionate about going out into all the world to reach a lost and broken people.

It's people who need to be purposefully recognized. When it comes to fulfilling our role as an ambassador or preacher or teacher, what—or who—are we pouring into? As we become filled by the Holy Spirit, overflowing with an endless tap of grace, what do we do with it? Drink ourselves into a holy stupor? (Forgive the analogy. Also, I hope you answered no.)

Purpose has no point if we only affect ourselves.

For example, we may be gifted at speaking. Our words can have profound effects on our listeners . . . but if we are doing these things to promote ourselves, can we really say we have fulfilled our purpose? If we know the truth that will set the longing soul free but keep it to ourselves, what good is that? Won't we be held accountable, both for the things we did and for the things we *didn't* do?

James 4:17 tells us "Whoever knows the right thing to do and fails to do it, for him it is sin." Matthew 25:45 states, "Then he will answer them saying, 'Truly I say to you, as you did not do it to one of the least of these, you did not do it to me.'"

If loving people means seeing them in the shadow of the cross, giving them the benefit of the doubt, and loving them like Jesus, it's easier to claim neutrality. It's easier to stay locked behind wooden doors and stone walls, living in my own beautiful world rather than pouring into someone else.

God knows we need rest. Our Savior went to the mountaintops alone to pray and fell asleep on a ship in the middle of a storm because he also needed rest. Yet when people needed healing, how many did he turn away? Comfort can be a tempting place to stay.

But maybe the comfortable life is missing something. Maybe the comfort is stifling, the thought of *I could do better* is lingering. Maybe God doesn't need another ambassador for the glorious kingdom to come. Be reminded of Moses, the stuttering, insecure leader who had massive amounts of people ridiculing him. Remember Paul in the prison cells.

This life and its glories are temporary; eternity is not.

I look back on my year of teaching and do not deny that it was hard. I am still (and probably always will be) baffled by those whose calling is to inspire the next generation. I believe teachers' souls are cut from fabrics of servitude, woven into radiant tapestries of hope and grace, but adorn the hallways that most people forget to walk. Family and close friends watched me unravel that year. I felt like a ghost of myself, cold and confused, unable to give my own strength because I didn't think it was what I was supposed to do. I felt blindsided. I didn't understand why the opportunity had presented itself to me or whether it was even from the Lord.

I certainly didn't endure the same physical and emotional pain as Paul. I've never gone without food or spent endless days in prison cells, nor have I found myself shipwrecked on foreign coasts or beaten with rods by my enemies. Unlike Paul, who experienced many sleepless nights, I've never gone more than a day without getting a chance to rest at some point.

I've been *uncomfortable.*

But I've never *suffered* like Paul.

But by the might and grace of the One who put me there—and despite my own doubt—miracles happened.

At the end of it, I knew God had called me to a parched land and told me to plant seeds. At the time, I expected a garden to be there already. Deserts aren't meant for planting seeds, but he does the impossible, doesn't he?

I'm no gardener, but the work isn't in my hands. It doesn't matter how well I can dig a hole. It's about obedience, about picking up a shovel and tossing the dirt over my shoulder simply because he told me to dig. It's about loving the souls he placed in my life not because they were easy to love, but because he gave me the job to care for them.

It's not even about knowing how many (if any) sprouts will shoot forth from the earth, whether I succeeded or failed—but whether I just *did* it.

That's how it is for us all. We could be in a desert or a garden, but there is still work to be done. It's work that involves people and vulnerability and restlessness and a myriad of other intricacies that are boring and beautiful and sometimes look anything but holy.

But in the end, despite all this and more, we know we lived for our King. We know we were obedient and loved when it felt impossible. And with assurance, we know he will be with us every step of the way, carrying us when it is too heavy, reflecting light and beauty off the dusty Damascus road.

9

What We Do With Who We Are

*"But each of you has your
own gift from God; one has this gift,
another has that." (1 Corinthians 7:7 NIV)*

There may have been one other small reason I couldn't seem to settle on what to study in college. Although I started out pursuing sociology (because I thought I wanted to become a social worker), I discovered I also really liked the idea of being an English professor. I somehow curated a vision that involved me carrying a brown leather briefcase across a university campus where I would lecture on the dynamics of the green light in *The Great Gatsby* and spend my free time eating apples and writing novels.

After about five minutes of careful thought and deliberation, I switched from sociology to English.

I thoroughly enjoy research. When it came to my career, it wasn't enough simply to pick something that I thought I might enjoy and stick with it. Even though I felt settled on what I was supposed to do, I began to question whether a career as an English professor would support me (or my dreams):

What if I can't make it as an English professor?

What if I can't find a job?

What else can I do with an English degree?

It was a nice dream, a beautiful one, even—but was it realistic? Could I really spend eight hours a day lecturing on novels I loved and scribbling away in an office somewhere and wandering the halls of an old university?

Would I be able to find full-time work?

Would I shrink at the idea of lecturing (a.k.a. public speaking)?

Would I need to pursue a doctorate in order to teach, and if so, would I be able to find a position that paid off all those student loans?

Suddenly the questions came in overwhelming waves and everything felt too complicated again. Maybe pursuing something I was passionate about wasn't the right idea, either.

I began researching jobs in the medical field. Many of my peers were going to nursing school. I loved the idea of working in pediatrics, or maybe even in the cardio thoracic department.

But the questions returned. Certainly, a nursing job would pay the rent and give me a hot meal at night and allow me to go out every now and then.

It would be stable, but would it be fulfilling in the ways I'd needed?

So, I moved on to the next idea. And then the next. And the next.

Thus began the spiraling into a number of different majors until I pretty much exhausted all my options (and my family members, for that matter). I ended up choosing (and somehow remained with) psychology. Because what better way to solve all your problems than helping people with theirs?

Somehow, I hoped there was a reason (or maybe many) for all of this erratic pendulum swinging.

Was I bored?

Afraid of hard work?

Fearful of not having enough financial stability?

Did I have too many passions?

I could probably answer yes to all of the above. But regardless of what career I chose, commitment would inevitably play a role, and maybe that's what scared me. Staying in one place for the rest of my life just didn't seem fulfilling. It felt a lot less like *living* and a lot more like *settling*.

I was chasing after things that I thought would be simultaneously stable and fulfilling. For a long time, I thought I needed to find a job that was going to make me happy, only to be told repeatedly by a number of people that work wasn't supposed to make me happy. It was work. Work pays the bills and allows one to enjoy the preciously short weekends and maybe a vacation once a year.

I didn't buy it.

I don't particularly agree or disagree with either side. I believe we can be passionate about our jobs, but I also believe that can be difficult to achieve. I've never identified the exact statistics, but from what I've gathered in my research, most people are somewhat unhappy in their jobs.

Still, I enthusiastically believe it's possible to love your work. And I think it all has to do with understanding our personal gifts and chasing hard and fast after them.

What I didn't believe as a young college student was that I could make a living as a writer and missionary. Only after college, when I was in the middle of jobs that would leave me in a melancholy state Sunday evening, did I really have the faith to believe it would all work out.

My flesh was tempted to contemplate the importance of employee benefits, medical insurance, and of course, financial compensation. Did missionaries get 401(k) plans? Did writers really make less than $10,000 a year?! How did it all work?

Still, I refused to settle into a mediocre life. I knew writing and ministry were what I wanted to make my life about.

To me, *that* was living.

I believe God plants dreams in our hearts. They can be life-altering or moment-changing. Writing a novel or starting an Etsy business. I relate it to the stirring that so many of us often feel, the "thing" that is prompting us to pursue something different, or something more. Not necessarily in an unhappy sense, but more along the lines of divine discontent. That is, something that is pushing us to do something more with what we are given.

I read a story not too long ago about a young German boy who fell in love with the bells of St. Anne's church. Every morning, he would stand on the street corner and stare up at the tower, listening and dreaming of one day ringing the bells himself. While most children have goals of becoming astronauts or dancers, this young man's dream was to become a bell ringer. Years later, he met and fell in love with a young German girl and told her about his dream. He led her up the 211 steps of the tower to the small apartment where the present bell ringers lived. The girl became afraid; to her, the tower looked more like a dungeon. She told the boy that she wanted to live in a normal house and have a normal life, and because the boy loved the girl, he complied.

Ten years after they were married, the girl was walking alone by the church of St. Anne's. She stared up at the beautiful tower where the bells rang. She began to realize living a normal life maybe wasn't as wonderful as she thought it would be. That night, she told the boy she wanted to live with him in the tower so he could fulfill his dream of being a bell ringer. According to the author, they are still living in the small apartment in the tower, ringing the bells to this day.[6]

Sometimes dreams can be a small part of our life.

Other times, they become our life.

Fulfilling them means stepping out and taking a risk. Often, it involves deliberate and purposeful praying. If the Lord is truly calling you to something with this dream that will not leave you alone, ask him to use it to impact the world.

---

[6] Sherry Ott, "A Story About Love and Bells," Ott's World, February 9, 2016, https://www.ottsworld.com/blogs/story-about-love-and-bells-saxony-germany/.

The knock on the door persists. It's gentle, it's soft, and it can be ignored and even missed . . . but it's there. And it does not stop.

Regardless, the dream (or the "calling") is the thing that you know you were meant to do. Maybe it means building a new career, maybe it's something that happens in addition to the rest of your life, maybe it's an ongoing project. Everyone is different.

But I'm assured we all have that one thing—a gift—that God has given to us personally as something only we can fulfill.

If you've grown up in church like I have, you've likely seen (or even taken) those questionnaires that determine what your spiritual gifts are. While those are helpful, that's not exactly what I'm talking about here. Some of those things (compassion, listening, speaking, etc.) fit into what I'm saying. But when I talk about gifts here, I mean *talents*.

I've known people who have used their gifts (or talents) and made careers out of them. One of my friends knew she was called to be a junior high teacher. (As a former teacher, I made quite a few teacher friends.) It's an age that most people would deem difficult, but she loves that age and can't imagine doing anything else. Aside from loving her job, she is one of the godliest women I know, and her career is also a ministry.

Another one of my friends—a fellow writer—is passionate about words and books and all things nostalgia. She opened up her own bookstore in our small town and now runs a small business. She's managed to combine her love of literature with her love for Jesus, and her career could be a ministry too.

But not all of us may find careers we might deem fulfilling or even enjoyable. Some of us may not even have careers at all.

I used to go to church with a woman who my friends and I looked up to. At one time, she ran the women's ministry in our church, but stepped down due to some family issues that pulled her into an extremely difficult season. During this season, she found herself changing jobs often. She didn't have a set career for a while. However, no matter which job she was at, she managed to bring the light of Jesus to her co-workers, clients, or staff. I can't pinpoint exactly what her gifts might have been, but I know she just shined Jesus' love. She was never afraid to bring up his name in a conversation or to share her personal struggles. She was a truly gentle and beautiful soul who managed to hold her head up high regardless of the stones that had been thrown in her path.

When we talk about gifts, it's important that we realize sometimes it's *not* about making a career out of them. Sometimes we can't.

In the Bible, there are countless verses regarding gifts:

"As each has received a gift, use it to serve one another, as good stewards of God's varied grace" (1 Pet. 4:10 ESV).

"Having gifts that differ according to the grace given to us, let us use them . . . if service, in our serving" (Rom. 12:6–7 ESV).

"For you were called to freedom, brothers. Only do not use your freedom as an opportunity for the flesh, but through love, serve one another" (Gal. 5:13 ESV).

Service: the common theme running through each verse. Our gifts aren't necessarily to market ourselves, or escalate our careers, or even grow our online platforms. They are there to *serve others*. 1 Corinthians 12:4–6 sums this up:

"Now there are varieties of gifts, but the same Spirit; and there are varieties of service, but the same Lord; and there are varieties of activities, but the same God who empowers them all in everyone." (ESV)

The point is this: we have established earlier that, as believers, we are called to actively spread the Word of God to all nations, starting with our neighbors, and then out to all the world.

Now how can we do that most effectively?

If someone is gifted with hospitality, would they most effectively use their gifts by traveling the globe presenting TED Talks or by opening up their own home to fellowship and Bible studies?

If someone else is gifted with loving children, would they best fit in a corporate office or in a classroom?

Regardless, we can use any gift we possess for any career. An individual with a hospitality gift can most certainly do TED Talks and people who love children can work in a corporate office. Theoretically, someone can use *any* spiritual gifting in any career if their primary goal is to be an ambassador for Christ. Our careers and gifts do not have to contradict; nor do they have to fall in line perfectly.

Sometimes they do, and other times they don't. This walk does not look the same for everyone. There are seasons where we may find ourselves in places we most certainly didn't ask for. But that doesn't make it any less glorious or purposeful.

I've seen—and personally experienced—what it's like to work in a place you are not suited for. It's not only draining, but demotivating.

After my year of teaching, I determined I needed a break from (may the Lord forgive me) people. And kids. I had already faced a room full of teenagers; now I could do anything.

And anything it was.

By some crazy spur-of-the-moment need to change my life, I applied and accepted a job in a ritzy little law firm, working as a legal assistant.

How much experience did I have filing papers, drafting summons, taking orders to court, and entering attorney time when I first started the job?

Absolutely none.

And afterward?

Still pretty much none, although now I know what litigation means (kind of) and I made friends with the security guards at the courthouse. (Oh, and lawyers love wine.)

I did learn a few things about myself: my name is on an eviction notice that was probably served to some homeless folks in the early winter of 2021, and I hate that; I really don't know what to say to lawyers during their after-hours wine and cheese parties; and working in a law firm was the equivalent of getting a root canal done eight hours every day.

So, I went back to what I knew: people.

Countless mornings, I would wake in the dark before I had to leave to sit at my desk and answer phone calls and enter time and make trips down to the courthouse. With a cup of coffee in one hand and my phone in the other, I sat and searched for other jobs close to home and in my field.

In some ways, I felt like a failure. In the past year, I'd had several jobs, and now here I was, quitting again and looking for another.

The days passed, and I didn't find anything that seemed like a fair balance—something that would leave me fulfilled but not completely drained. In the evenings, I lay in my bed and told the Lord how much I would love to go back to working with people, maybe even serving the families of this community that I had once loathed but had now come to love.

In the spring, I received a call back from a social services position I'd applied for. It was working with child welfare cases and families in need. I had already called twice and left several messages but hadn't heard back, so I assumed I'd been overlooked.

"We would like for you to come in for an interview," the receptionist told me. "What is a good day and time?"

That week I went in and interviewed during my lunch.

The next week, I got a text message from the company asking me to come in for a second interview.

I thought that was bad news. "They're probably trying to decide between me and someone else," I told my mom. I knew they would be watching me even more closely. If I messed this up or said the wrong thing, it meant more weeks or even months at the law firm.

The pressure seemed to be more elevated than the previous interview, and I knew it was because I wanted it. I wanted this position in a small corner of my small town, serving the families of this community.

It was galaxies away from the law firm, and that felt perfect.

As I walked in, the receptionist handed me the same set of questions I'd looked at the week before when I'd first interviewed. I was confused. Why were they asking me these again?

"Oh wait," she told me after a few moments. "You were here last week, correct?"

"Yeah," I nodded, laughing nervously. Maybe they wouldn't want to interview me again after all. Could it be a mistake?

"Yeah, you can go on up." I followed another girl into the elevator, and she showed me to the room where I would have the second interview.

I didn't have time to review the set of questions they set in front of me, but I suppose it wasn't necessary. That evening, I got a call from the program director informing me the position was mine. She ended the voicemail asking me when I could start.

I gave my two weeks' notice at the law firm the next day.

The job I accepted then has carried me through until now. Though the work is hard, I leave my office more fulfilled because I know I am doing the work for which God has created me. It's not easy. It's often so awful that my co-workers and I have to laugh because it's better to laugh eight hours a day than to cry. In the midst of sorrow, we brainstorm and write reports and think of the small ways we can find joy in the fragmented parts of human suffering.

Sometimes it gets to me. No one can listen to the unthinkable horrors of neglect and drugs and abuse and see the way it affects both children and adults, then go home on a Friday night unscathed. Many evenings, I go home unwilling to feel carefree and unbothered because I'm terribly burdened. I have unexplained anxiety that rears its ugly head on a Saturday afternoon in an In-N-Out drive thru. I worry now more than I ever used to.

Yet I can honestly say that doing what I'm doing is so much more fulfilling to me than all the comforts of my English professor dreams. Because the world hurts. Society is suffering. People are so full of pain that when you try to help them, they wrestle with the outstretched hands that offer hope.

But God has shown up in so many ways: when a family is reunited; when an addicted mother gets clean; or when suffering children are adopted by a family ready to take on the weight of their life story.

And through the trials and glories of this job, I can say this is—undoubtedly—what I was created to do.

Is it what I would have chosen?

Absolutely not.
But I'm so thankful God chose me for it.

Part III
Walking in Love

McKenna Vietti

10

God's Heart Beats for People

"Let us love one another." (1 John 4:7 NIV)

I'm a lover of words. Because so many of our English words stem from Greek and Hebrew, and because God's Word was written in those languages, I'm also very much in love with them. (I have yet to become fluent in either. Maybe in heaven?)

When I was in my early twenties, my Christmas wish was to own this thick, brown Greek and Hebrew Bible translation that my church sold in its bookstore. In the early winter of 2020, I bought my first Hebrew book by Dave Adamson, *52 Hebrew Words Every Christian Needs to Know.* I also never forgave my university for not offering a study of the original Greek Scriptures. (Go Red Hawks anyway, I guess.)

I fell in love with the Greek language in mid-spring 2014. My mom and my seventeen-year-old self were sitting in my parents' beige Taurus in the parking lot of a little breakfast and lunch bistro called *Huckleberry's*. I was sitting in the passenger seat, clutching my little resume with sweaty hands, wondering if I would ever make it inside. Before I walked in to speak with the manager, my mom pointed out the license plate on one of the other cars. It read: AGAPE.

On the drive home, she explained to me what it meant. Agape was love, but not the kind of love I longed for as a teenager (perhaps because I thought another person would make me whole). It's not the kind of love that exists in novels and fairytale romances and Taylor Swift songs. It's not the love that puts one's own needs and wants first, or the unmistakable on-fire feelings that come from simply being in the presence of someone else.

Agape is so much more.

Agape is the love that God has for his children. It is the kind of love that selflessly chooses someone else over and over. The entire thirteenth chapter of 1 Corinthians exemplifies this kind of love. It's a patient, kind, selfless, slow to anger, rich in hope and goodness, devoted to the other person kind of love.

It's the kind of love God has for us.

And it's the kind of love he expects us to have for each other.

(Also, I did get the job . . . if you were wondering.)

Opportunities to apply this love have been numerous. I'm still learning to understand it, and have been for years, and one of the first moments of learning how to live it came to me in January 2020. I was sitting with a wise, older friend inside a teal-tiled room at Murietta Bible College. The outline of a dove was engraved over the stage where the speaker was bringing to life words and concepts that my young mind had never conceived.

I hurriedly wrote everything down. My pen would not move as quickly as I needed it to, and I was terrified I would miss some vital truth.

Our speaker's name was Leona Karni. She had been a missionary most of her life. She'd met and known and loved a lot of people and written several books. I presumed they told compelling tales of her life and adventures overseas, of lessons she'd learned along the way and the beautifully broken people she'd met and ministered to. She had traveled through the seas of Thailand and the red roads of other countries and somehow wound up at a Bible college in Southern California, inspiring an eager twenty-something who marveled at how she fulfilled her purpose so clearly. Every day must have been an adventure for her as she taught the Word of God to a nation that may not otherwise have known it.

That was *prothesis*—to be set forth to do something exceptionally wonderful for the Kingdom of God.

I wanted to live that life so badly.

But she was not speaking of purpose now. Instead, she posed a question to the audience of women, none of whom had an answer for her. "What if our words," she asked, "remain long after we've said them?"

I wrote her question down, but in my head I thought *Remain? Like, literally?*

Our speaker described a theory that I'd never heard before, nor would ever hear the same way again. *What if our words continue to exist?* she asked us. What if every word we've ever said out loud—the prayers, the gossip, the lies we told when we didn't want to face the truth, the cries we've sputtered after disappointment, the murmurings, the *I don't love you*'s and the *I'm sorry*'s, the elegant prose and the horrible things we thought no one could hear because we muttered them under our breath—what if all of that remained? *Literally?*

In theory, she told us, it was possible. She went on to discuss a sound wave resonator that was used to store quantum data. Theoretically, all the words that have ever been spoken could be decoded and stored and kept through the years to come. Our words would never cease to exist.

As she spoke, her words became long streams of scientific jargon that my literary mind struggled to follow; but what I did catch was a bizarre idea that had never been presented to me before: what would happen if I could see my words transcribed on pages and pages before me? What if each sentence I said, every word I spoke, found a home on the walls of my house? Would it matter if I decorated with Persian carpets and silk drapes to add to the beauty of my words?

Would I need thicker carpets to cover the ugliness that so frequently escaped my mouth?

My takeaway was the simple truth that we are taught in grade school yet forget to take seriously: words hurt. Whether we say them to each other in the heat of an argument or cut someone up behind their back, what's the long-term impact? Are they being stored away somewhere in the universe? Are they being recorded on the walls of our homes and churches and workplaces only to one day be decoded?

Our words have a greater and more prolonged effect than many of us realize. What we say, over and over, is a reflection of what is going on in our hearts and minds:

"The good person out of the good treasure of his heart produces good, and the evil person out of his evil treasure produces evil, for out of the abundance of the heart his mouth speaks" (Luke 6:45 ESV).

There are so many ways to love. But if what we're saying to and about each other isn't matching up with what God tells us to do, are we truly loving? Our actions can say one thing, but what about when the crowd has left? When the lights are no longer lit, when the sun sets and we are alone with our thoughts and maybe one or two close friends or family members, are we still careful with what we say?

My emphasis on this is great, probably because I need it more than anyone. I can wake up urging myself not to let my mouth have its own way, but all I have to do is log into social media or check in with a friend or family member, and pretty soon the insensitive words have left my mouth before I remember that I'm supposed to *love* people today.

Our words are powerful. Proverbs 18:21 states that death and life are in the power of the tongue. Proverbs 12:18 reminds us that rash words are like sword thrusts. Jesus tells us in Matthew 12:37 that by our words will we be condemned. He also says in Matthew 12:36 that on the day of judgment, people will have to account for every careless word they speak.

I think that's the problem for many of us. Perhaps it's not so much that we long to cut someone else down behind their back, but we carelessly share something that is likely to be both unconfirmed and untrue.

If our words have this much power (and they do), what care we must take with what comes out of our mouths. Our words can theoretically withstand the stains of the ages and wrinkles of time. They have the power to destroy life or renew it. They are a blade slicing through flesh and balm to the most painful of wounds.

We can speak the Word of God over those who come into our life, whether they are there forever or merely a chapter, whether they encourage us or God uses them to polish our sharp edges. By our words, we can break down walls. By our words, we can bring healing.

By our words, can we love.

I almost wish it was as easy as that.

Many of us know how to be cordial to someone's face. I may wave as I pass certain people on the sidewalk or offer a smile at church or a farmers' market. And yet, as soon as they've left my sight, I'm tempted to think of all the ways they've wronged me or how our past isn't as pristine as it should be. I reflect on how difficult it is to love not only while they're standing in front of me, but to speak of them in my prayers and not to someone else who will join me in my disdain. As the psalmist prayed for the Lord to put a guard over his mouth, (Psalm 141:3) so will I, although a muzzle may be more appropriate in my case. Lord help me.

But even if I can become a master controller, what's truly going on in my heart?

How do you love someone you don't even *like*?

If purpose is fulfilled through imitating Christ and being an ambassador for him and loving not only the sinners of the world but also the difficult-to-love brothers and sisters of the church, can purpose still be fulfilled even if there are people I just don't get along with? If I can be sweet to people while they are standing in front of me, while my thoughts are racing on a track that is the polar opposite of what I'm supposed to be thinking, how am I really loving?

It's overwhelming. None of us are perfect, and we all need the intervention of the Lord in order to do this.

Lately, I've been reading and learning more about the brain. Because of the nature of my job, it's beneficial for me to understand how it works, how it stores memory, how it develops, how we learn, and so forth. In my research, I have discovered one baffling thing that lines up with Scripture so well it's almost hilarious.

Our brain consists of several parts. Within those parts are little excitable cells called neurons that are responsible for sending messages to the brain. When these cells connect, they are called synapses. Synapses are, from what I understand, basically little pathways for these neurons to transmit messages. Early experiences shape these pathways. For example, a child that is born in a warm, loving, and caring home is going to have different synapses than a child who experienced trauma at an early age.

What's interesting and a relatively new discovery (at least for me) is that the brain can *change*. For many people, this is incredibly hopeful and exhilarating news. If one's childhood was stolen from them, or if depression was once your master, breaking free is a reality. Early experiences do not have to claim you. And if early experiences do not have to claim you, early impressions do not, either.

How is this possible? By a phenomenon scientists call neuroplasticity. Like its name suggests, it's basically a remolding of the brain. While most of us already know that the brain is not made of plastic, we may not realize that it's *moldable*. Since this phenomenon emphasizes the brain's responsibility in learning and memory, it is possible to "rewire" those synapses by reorganizing the connections. For those whose early connections may have been based in fear, abuse, and neglect, this means that the brain can be rewired so the default response won't be the same as someone who has encountered trauma.[7]

How does it work?

Neuroplasticity can be maintained in a number of ways: physical exercise, enriching oneself in stimulating environments and activities (such as learning a new language), and what I believe to be the most important one of all: practicing and repeating positivity. Just as one can learn a new habit after mindfully practicing it for a certain number of days, you can literally rewire your brain to be more posi- tive just by practicing positivity.

I believe that this is what Paul meant when he wrote about renewing our mind (Romans 12:2) and taking our thoughts captive (2 Corinthians 10:5). When we *continually* fix our minds on God and carefully choose our thoughts, we are consequently rewiring our brain to be in a more holy and pleasing state.

When we study, meditate on, and memorize Scriptures, the words of God will engrave themselves upon our hearts and minds.

When we decide to think positively of a person, to pray for them continually, to stop allowing ourselves to gossip or cut them down behind their back, we can eventually learn to love them in the way God commands us. We have to work at it, and make the conscious decision to think these thoughts, but I believe it's indeed possible.

Like Agape, it is a *choice*.

As a result, we will no longer have to gossip, nor will we require a guard over our mouth. Instead, we can sing beautiful things over those we probably couldn't imagine *truly* loving. God has given us the ability to exercise our

---

[7] "Neuroplasticity," *Psychology Today*, accessed May 17, 2022, https://www.psychologytoday.com/us/basics/neuroplasticity.

brains, the power of words, and plenty of people to practice on.

It seems that no matter how many times I ask for forgiveness, and no matter how often I ask the Lord to help me love and see people the way he does and put a guard over my mouth (that most definitely has its own mind), I still can't seem to speak in a way that edifies the specific people I struggle to love.

Maybe I'm comparing myself.

Maybe unrealistic expectation is the underlying thief of joy.

Maybe we're all stuck between where we were and where we want to be, with our hearts begrudgingly reminding us of all the people who have wronged us for allegedly "no reason at all" so that we can't seem to move on.

But the inability to speak well of others—regardless of whether we can be sweet to their face or not—is like a poison that rots us from the inside out.

I can't help but remember some of the people who used to be in my life but then drifted out because our hearts were unwilling to forget the wrongs of the past. If I'd made it a goal to speak lovingly and pray over them as I prayed for everyone and everything else in my life, would it have made a difference?

Years ago, I met someone who I believed would be a lifelong friend. At the time, we were both living in our parents' homes, scraping through community college, and dreaming about weddings and moving out. We did Bible studies and prayed together and took trips to the city and explored the downtown, conversing about life and people and how strangely beautiful it was to grow up and find yourself in a place you never would have imagined.

I don't remember exactly what changed between us, or when. But even the best of friends need space from each other, and we didn't realize that . . . so we didn't have any. Our time together grew to be almost suffocating. Neither of us realized we were drowning until it was too late.

Our relationship became more and more strained until we finally broke. Over text one day, my friend prodded me with questions regarding a recent incident between myself and someone I had been talking to. I wasn't ready to talk about what had happened. I ignored her questions as long as I could, but when she refused to stop, my thumbs frantically typed away a message that was anything but loving.

Among other things, she had asked what had happened so she could pray. In so many words, I abruptly informed her that what had happened was none of her business and I didn't appreciate her "poking around for information."

It took several months for us to finally start talking again, but we never fully discussed the issue that broke us. While we still talk occasionally, the damage of unloving words and the refusal to resolve what happened left us both hurt and confused.

Because of it, we missed out on milestones in each other's lives—marriages, moves, graduations—that we thought we would share.

There is no place in our lives for unloving words. While there will be times we are all prone to let our words slip, we should be quick to catch ourselves, apologize, and try to do better. I believe that if I had waited to press send, or turned my phone off, or tried to apologize a little sooner and not let myself marinate in the ugliness, we might still have the friendship we once did.

If we are to be imitators of Christ, we need to choose to obey this less than pleasant command: love one another. Flesh devours gossip but repels the spirit. I don't love everyone perfectly. I'm still working on loving a few.

But what a world it would be if all Christians took seriously the command to love.

11

Salt and Light

I am still learning how to love.

Like many of us, I know how to love when it's easy: when I meet a co-worker whose sense of humor and growing process is similar to mine; when I see Christ through a soul who has experienced the depths of heartbreak and depression and has turned the broken pieces into a mosaic; when my brothers and sister and I pile into my Mustang at the end of a long day and go for drives while I vent away the stress of living in a world that doesn't make sense.

Like the ones I trusted with my dreams, ambitions, and secrets only to have them abuse and twist the truth of situations. Or the sisters in Christ who I've partnered with in ministry until competition drove us apart. It's the woman who opened her home to me but then drove me away through petty remarks and cold stares. It's others, too, when our history was before us, and there were no cuts or bruises. Nostalgia causes me to look back at the past to a time when nothing hurt. It seems no amount of prayer or poetry or positive thinking will take away the painful sensations that always seem to linger in the depths—that surge during the less-than-beautiful moments of truth.

But what is love if I'm selective with it? If we are to be true ambassadors, representing Christ in a world where everything else seems cold, we can't just believe we are supposed to love people.

We need to obey.

Love me. (Matt. 22:37)

Love people. (v.39)

Go out into all the world and preach the Gospel, making disciples of all nations. (Matt. 28:19)

It wasn't just Jesus' brothers and sisters he so freely loved but also the Samaritan woman. The man who tore chains apart and lived in tombs. The beggars on dusty roadsides. The thieves who clung tightly to gold coins but even tighter to him. The ones who ate with him, whose feet he washed hours before a devastating betrayal that led to a gruesome death.

I can't imagine loving someone so two-faced. I'm ready to type up words that explain the truth about everything so the world will know how I've been wronged. But just before I hit post, I'm reminded of who he's created me to be, and how he's told me to live.

He cups my face with his nail-scarred hands and tells me softly that he doesn't just *understand* the pain of betrayal, but experienced it on a level I can hardly imagine. And gently he prods me to drop the stones and wash their feet.

If you love me, you will obey my commands. (Jn. 14:15)

My hands tremble, the stones fall, and I do my best to obey.

It sounds simple, and it should be, but the complexity of our humanity complicates everything. Sometimes our personalities don't jive with others'. Anger, competition, drama, and gossip drown out the sweet whisper of our Savior who commands us to love one another.

Not *just* the easy to love but also the ones whose words stung with lies and lingered in betrayal. The ones who took everything you were reaching for and seem not only to be thriving but also blissfully unaware of what they've done to you.

These are the people who were supposed to stand with you, not over you.

Even them, Lord?

Yes, love even them. Give them food. Quench their thirst. Wash their feet.

After all, didn't Jesus do this and more?

In the ragged edges of humanity, we find the Judases and Mary Magdalenes and a reasonable amount of Pharisees. When we look at them, it's difficult to see past the sin. If only we could choose to become blinded by the goodness of others rather than overlook it because their transgressions seem too bold to ignore.

Or maybe sometimes we struggle to love others because, as we gaze upon their iniquities, our own reflection burns back.

Maybe in order to love as Christ does, we need to understand how he first loved us.

I look back and see souls who were so difficult to show any love to. It's hard to give love to those who won't accept it. After all, how possible is it to love those who never seem to love (or even like) me back no matter how many different ways I've tried to rebuild the bridges?

But I also look back and see the girl with chocolate brown skin that contrasted so strongly with my ivory tone. She loved my T-shirt, and I loved her dress. Angel was seventeen but seemed years older, probably because in her short years, she'd seen more pain and sorrow in her little Honduran village than most people see in a lifetime. I see Olest, the young translator who dreamed of someday going to college. Together, we'd sing hymns as he taught me how to shovel and sift sand beneath a sweltering Haitian sun. I think of the countless men and women whose sweat dripped from brows in suffocating humidity while they carried cement stones up dirt roads to provide shelter for their families. Co-workers who accepted me with open arms. These people remain so clearly in my memory because we *did* love each other. Despite the imperfections, disagreements, and sin, regardless of the differences in cultures, lives, and beliefs, we became grafted together. In those moments of working side-by-side—under the sun or in an office—it didn't matter what our differences were, because our love united us.

The disciple John knew this kind of love. He made it his final mission to tell the world of this love. He knew what it looked like to love the Judases and the Peters, the Samaritan women and the Mary Magdalenes, the haters in the street who spit on your face and those who betray you for some silver. John watched Love ride down dusty Galilean roads and touch the bodies of the ones whose skin was falling off and cleanse the minds of the mentally insane and finally run crimson down a cedar cross on a horrific spring afternoon.

This son of thunder, this burly fisherman who gutted animals and slept in boats was so overwhelmed by this love that knew no bounds, he couldn't help but preach it until his final breath.

In 1 John, he writes about a new commandment: the commandment to love one another. Not the world, but those who are in the world.

It was a revelation that hit me after being on my Christian walk for what seemed like a long time. We are not supposed to love this world the way we are supposed to love the people in it. It's easy to be captivated by the glorious creation: the snowy cliffs, balmy emerald jungles, and sparkling desert sands. Even endangered animals seem to capture our souls more than the millions of orphan children starving in impoverished countries.

Yet how can we not look at another human and see the cross? We are mirrored in the eyes of others, yet our response is so often to turn away, indifferent. Indifference is the opposite of what Jesus urged and what John and so many others spent their lives trying to teach.

In Haiti, I was fulfilled.

On the sixth or seventh day, we rose in the dark to drink black coffee and eat breakfast to strengthen us for the work ahead. The work consisted of building walls and loving children, praying over nursing mothers, carrying dry cement up mountains, painting desks for the schoolroom, or walking teenagers (and sometimes, ourselves) to the compound's clinic.

In the afternoon, I took my Bible and my journal and walked to the rooftop alone. I began to write of how I knew—I just *knew*—God was calling me to be a missionary. My twenty-two-year-old self read through the end of Matthew, where Jesus told his disciples to go into all the world and make disciples, and I thought, *This is me. This is my purpose. This is why God created me.*

In an instant, I saw myself one day coming back to Haiti, or Honduras, or somewhere else where I felt fulfilled because no matter what I was doing, whether it was using my hands to shovel dirt or touch a sick child, I *felt* so purposeful. There, the work was meaningful, the people were easy to love, and the world was a mission field.

But in less than two years, I graduated from college. And while I would find myself doing similar work—praying over individuals, using my words to encourage, and listening to the grieving hearts—I wasn't overseas in a red-dirt country.

It was in a small office with no windows where I case managed and listened and counseled. Where I had to learn, once again, to cling to grace and the hem of his garment. I repeated the Scripture that promises plans over purpose, to the hope that Jesus gives us so much to live for.

Again, I found myself rising early in the morning, hours before the sun would peek over the Northern California mountaintops. Each morning I'd rush downstairs to make that first cup of coffee, then drive thirty miles down an empty highway, pull off past dark fields and into a cramped parking lot where I would sit in my car and reread the 119th Psalm, hoping it would saturate my heart enough, so I could make it through another day. Maybe I could, again, pray for the strength to pour into the souls God had allowed into my life. I felt so defeated, but what have I got to complain about, when half the people I talked to every day struggled with addictions, homelessness, and worse? I remember the mornings I would fumble with my keys in the dark, let myself into the building, and sit inside my suffocating little office. On numerous occasions, I would find the medical assistants had double booked me again; I didn't think I could do this job.

This space felt empty and foreign—more distant than the Central American soil I still dream about. That was where I wanted to be.

In this space, I lacked fulfillment. Everything seemed to be smothering me. In this new land of a workplace, some-thing inside me whispers that it's not supposed to be this way, but it isn't reassuring. What can I really do to change it at this point? Do I really leave a good job and needy souls just because it feels . . . boring?

Had the dream of being a missionary been just an illusion? Wasn't changing the world supposed to feel more exciting than this?

I scan my list of patients. At a glance, they look like nothing more than words on a page, but most of them are struggling with homelessness and meeting their counseling increments for the month. Most of them will respond with one-word answers when I call them up to ask about their treatment and recovery.

But then I see the name of my third patient for that morning. He was one I always used to dread calling for counsel because during his first several sessions, he would scream profanities, blaming me for not being granted his take home medication or problems with testing or being forced to attend counseling. There were times I was short back. But after learning to exercise some form of patience, and learning to ask the right questions, he now looks forward to our sessions.

At least that was something.

But maybe the problem isn't the job, or the career, or where I am in life.

Maybe it is me, sitting there, feeling less and less like myself because my energy is depleted once again. My emotions are overwhelming, and yet I feel numb, unable to give anymore. Though many days I come home with the unmistakable belief that I've accomplished something and ministered to someone, I don't know if I have the mental and emotional capacity to wake up and do it all again. Monday mornings find me nearly in tears before my first patient.

Wasn't *anything* other than teaching supposed to be better?

It's easy—and maybe even okay—to want the mountaintops; but if it's just the mountaintops we're living for, then *who* are we living for? Church planting is exciting. Leading souls to Christ is exhilarating. Who wants to fill jars of clay when you can watch mountains move? If it is up to me, I want to go where things happen on a big scale. If I'm going to live radically, change better be happening every single day, where I can *see* it.

Oh, how I can almost hear my Father say, *you of little faith.*

How can we think anything he does through us is *ever* insignificant?

As Christians, do we really want the thousand fed or do we want the glory of the miracle? It's easy to want the big things when splendor follows. If we think glorious outcomes are going to follow us after doing the Lord's work—whether it's leading a thousand souls to him or planting a hundred churches—it's easy to want to live every day for Christ.

Had someone told Jeremiah that after forty years of preaching he would have led no one to repentance, would he have continued? Would he have had the motivation? Or would he do it regardless of his own personal feelings, simply because the Lord told him to?

I say this because, over the years, I've had to rethink my own motives for doing work in the name of Christ. Was I going on this mission trip because I wanted to serve these people, or was I thrilled at the idea of experiencing a different culture? Was I really committed to being a missionary, or was I committed to the idea of an intrepid life?

I once had a missionary boldly tell me to lower my expectations and rethink my "dreams" of mission work. I may have blocked out his exact words, but his message was clear: *stop getting your hopes up.* At the time, I couldn't imagine why someone would want to shoot down a young person's well-meaning dreams. Now, I appreciate the candor, because this Christian life doesn't always consist of romanticized adventures.

This walk is work that can look boring to an outsider (or a hopeful twenty-two-year-old).

As I've said, I've learned; but I'm still learning.

I'm learning that being salt and light in a world of tasteless darkness is more than sharing the gospel message every day to every single person I meet. It's about the relationships I build with co-workers, letting them witness my lifestyle before I whisper the story of love and grace. It is about the patients I pray for within my stifling little office. It's about the children I get to love, and the parents I have the privilege to teach and empower.

The opportunities to love abound around us. If loving means washing the feet of my enemies, what does it look like for the strangers on the street?

I think back to the woman I saw countless times in front of the local grocery store. She was holding a cardboard sign and sitting on the parking lot curb with a baby in her lap. In broken English, she tells her story of a husband who walked away from their four children and left her to pay the rent.

Does love turn away?

Does it give her money?

Does it question a possibly fraudulent story, because certainly love doesn't get taken advantage of?

Or maybe love chooses to serve without having to know every detail.

Maybe love is going back inside the store and praying that God will direct you to the right product that will not only nourish her and her child, but maybe offer them something they haven't been able to afford for a while.

But love wouldn't stop there.

Love would serve both her body and her soul.

Love would ask her if she knows Jesus and say a prayer and remind her that she is loved by El Roi, the God who sees her in her lonely helplessness.

While in Zarephath, Elijah didn't just tell the widow she would have enough flour and oil to feed herself and her son for a single day.

"This is what the Lord, the God of Israel, says: 'The jar of flour will not be exhausted and the jug of oil will not run dry until the day the Lord sends rain upon the face of the earth'" (1 Kings 17:14 BSB).

Love doesn't just give someone bread when the real hunger comes from a supernatural place. More than the stomach, the soul and spirit need care and sustenance.

This is what the Lord says: he sees you and loves you and cares for you and your four children. He has plans and a purpose for you, if only you look to him and let him live in you.

If we are simply giving our human resources, we exhaust ourselves. Time, money, and strength diminish.

But when we allow the Lord to work through us, the jug of oil will not run dry.

To love him is to *serve* him.

To serve him is to *love* others.

To love others is to *serve* others.

This reminds me of Jesus' expectations of his disciples. We are to be called salt and light (Matt. 5:13–14)—to enhance the things, the people, and the environments around us. To add flavor. Create thirst. Emphasize what is already there. Part the curtains and let the truth shine through. We can't do any of this by sitting by the fireside, wishing our dreams would come true already. We need to go out and *live*, spreading the love and truth no matter what situation we are in.

We are not to be isolated. If the bottom line is people, what good are salt and light just for ourselves? I think back to the times in my life when I completely isolated myself from friends and other loved ones because I didn't want to contact anyone outside of work. I attributed this to being the introvert that I was. But having no contact with people and staying in my safe little introvert bubble left me feeling, in fact, quite miserable.

Avoidance is not an option. Jesus said we are the salt and light.

Light makes things visible. It reveals the reality of Christ's presence in our lives through worshiping, loving, and serving. The light is not our own, but a reflection of him.

In Philippians 2:15, the word for light is similar to the word for the beacon that a lighthouse emits.[8] A beacon is bright and unmistakable in its purpose: it warns of upcoming danger, directs one to a safe harbor, and provides hope. With this in mind, look around you. Billions of people today are completely lost and without hope. We are to be their light, that beacon that steers the lost and weary sailor home.

If we are not salt and light, we are being disobedient.

I've learned that this isn't limited to overseas. In the part of Northern California where I live, homelessness and substance abuse thrive. When we first moved to the Western town, I thought of it as an infestation. Now, all I can see is a mission field. There's so much to be done. When I think about how much he has called us to do, I feel lost in the swarms of people, but in the best way. It's a reminder that this world is so big, and I am so small, just a tiny vessel; but he's given me the power to do so much. How can we let day after day go by and not harness that power?

Peter writes that we are to fulfill our calling by making our lives about him (1 Peter 4:10-11). Reading our Bibles and going to church and praying in closets is good, but if we want to fulfill our purpose and live up to *prothesis* and everything it has to offer, sooner or later we need to leave the safety of our comfort zones and do *something*. Faith stirs us to works. There is a reason we feel restless.

We aren't supposed to just tell people or talk about it; *we are to make our lives about him.* It is a lifestyle that means getting our hands dirty as we're washing the feet of someone

---

[8] Strong's G5458. n.d. "phoster." Blue Letter Bible. accessed February 23, 2023, https://www.blueletterbible.org/lexicon/g5458/kjv/tr/0-1/.

else. So, shock the world and love your enemies. Make your life completely and utterly about Jesus. It doesn't mean you have to go on a hundred mission trips and sign up for Sunday school and attend all the Bible studies, but *go where he is leading you personally.* You can worship him by a well or a river. Sing the song of hope in the hills and the valleys, to the rich and to those without homes.

If we earnestly seek him, he promises he will be found (Jeremiah 29:13-14), and he will lead us to where we can love the most abundantly.

Something about knowing my Savior punctures holes in my heart. He fills me and then bleeds out onto the people I've struggled with loving. He strips away the sin that so easily entangles and reminds me that his children are all running the same race, only it doesn't matter at all who finishes first. It's about reaching the end. How much better would it be if we all helped each other along the way?

Every now and then, he pulls me away from the lens I usually look through to see people and gives me his eyes. I'm given only a glimpse—just enough to break my heart—but not so much that I'm overwhelmed with grief. In this temporary glance, the searing pain of humanity reminds me that we're all lost and confused children trying to find our way back home.

And this is what prompts me, over and over, to keep trying. I don't do it perfectly every day, if ever. But if I'm going to pick up stones, I'm moving them to clear the path of someone else. If I'm going to the trouble of washing my own feet, I may as well carry twice as much water.

Love stuns the enemy and awakens a sleeping soul. It doesn't begin or end with us because this kind of love can only come from allowing Jesus to shape your perspective and shift your gaze. When we see him, *prothesis* is fulfilled. We see who we are meant to be, and the essence of all we are called to do.

12

Living It Out

Several summers ago, I heard a message that penetrated my heart and gave more life to the message of this book.

I was sitting in a small church surrounded by a thick covering of thriving olive trees. The sun glowed orange and sunk behind cotton candy clouds. Something about the breeze always made words feel and sound more emphatic. I let the warmth of the summer day wash over me. Maybe I hadn't fallen in love with the heat, but I'd learned to bear it.

After all, without the heat, how would the olive trees thrive?

Inside, our speaker stood behind a shiny wood pulpit. A stained-glass cross shimmered vibrant shades behind her as she shared with us the work she'd been doing for the last two years while serving overseas at a Bible college. As per usual, I was scrawling notes in my Bible and on the backs of bulletins, wondering once again if I would ever serve in the ministry. My heart longed to go serve the world like the missionaries and teachers in Peru.

I am constantly being reminded of how being a missionary and working in the ministry is the life I want; yet somehow, I still feel so powerless to get there. I'm growing content with that—but my heart still somehow longs for it.

At the end of our speaker's message, she shared with us how she, too, had been wondering about purpose and where God was leading her next. She had so many questions about her own life, she finally brought everything to her mentor, the president of the Bible college.

His purpose seemed so clear and evident. When she brought her concerns to him, explaining that she wanted to feel settled and secure like he was, his response was simple:

"Every morning, I wake up and ask God, what shall I do for you?"

As she told us this story, those words answered the question I'd been asking myself for most of my life. The importance of obedience must be emphasized when one asks for God's will to be done. We must be open to what he is calling us to, and then be willing to *do it*.

What shall I do for you?

This day, what shall I do for you?

In this job, what shall I do for you?

Looking back, I can see how I *wasn't* open to other ideas for my life. My mind was so fixated on ministry and serving overseas that all I could think about was working in a church or being a missionary in another country. With steadfast certainty, I put everything I had into that dream, never once thinking God may have other plans for my life. I didn't plan on ever buying a house in the States. I wasn't about to marry anyone who wasn't willing to trek with me overseas. I wouldn't go back to school if it required me to stay in the Western town any longer than I had to. Consequently, I said no to a lot of things and a lot of people, simply because *my* ideas for my life fit into one particular box.

God undeniably put ministry in my heart, and, unbeknownst to me at the time, I have done it in a number of ways. I have been blessed with the privilege to travel, share, speak, and pray over many different types of people. God has allowed me to live so much life in the years I've been on this Earth. How could I not be overwhelmed with gratitude?

But for the Christian, ministry isn't about what you do every day; it's about how you *live*.

As I've said many times throughout this journey, we are called to so much more than a nine-to-five. We are ambassadors on a mission to tell a miserable world of a perfect Savior. When words aren't enough, we are called to live out this message. We need ambassadors everywhere: in the classroom, grocery stores, hospitals, corporate buildings, forests, prisons, and anywhere and everywhere else. We need them in the home, raising future ambassadors to courageously battle the trouble that lies ahead.

Some of us want adventure. And some of us enjoy the sweet taste of peace. As Christians, we can have a bit of both. Our lives do not have to be mundane.

With Jesus, we can do what he's prepared us for. You have to remember how set apart you are, to live this life that he called only *you* to live. It doesn't matter if you're bagging groceries or slinging coffee beans or mopping up spills or flying airplanes. We are each called according to his purpose. This is where he has you.

The only way we can live our best life is to live for him, no matter where he calls us.

As we reach for Jesus and chase hard after purpose, let us remember the words Paul wrote to the Romans in the church of Philippi:

> "Not that I have already obtained this or am already perfect, but I press on to make it my own, because Christ Jesus has made me his own. Brothers, I do not consider that I have made it my own. But one thing I do: forgetting what lies behind and straining forward to what lies ahead, I press on toward the goal for the prize of the upward call of God in Christ Jesus." (Phil. 3:12–15 ESV)

McKenna Vietti

Part IV
Settled Yet Unsettled

13

Mosaics

Sometimes, in the middle of heartbreak and disappointment, we learn to surrender.

This was another lesson that was difficult to learn. No matter how many times my dreams shattered before my eyes, I continued to restructure and reframe the pieces. A lot of it was rebuilding. Most of it was learning to take the shards and create something new, transforming the serrated edges into a mosaic of broken dreams.

Not too long ago, I learned about a Japanese art called *kintsugi.* It is a method that involves putting broken pottery pieces back together with gold. The technique is built upon the idea that even with our flaws, imperfections, and failures, we can be pieced back together more beautifully, in a way we never could have been if the cracks had never come to be.

I see God doing this with our dreams. I spent many years of my life thinking of how I should be or how I wanted my life to look.

Disappointment, hurt, and heartbreak often followed. Even as I dreamed and planned, I still prayed for God's will. Consequently, my will was dashed to pieces.

It hurts.

But somehow, despite the wreckage and desolation, there is a power and a magnificence that only the wind and rain can beget. In the whirring there is a hopelessness of trying to control what is not mine . . . and that is beautiful. Succumbing to the realization that we are not God is a form of holiness, and with that, I can acknowledge that the destruction of our lives can be beautiful.

When Christ's blood ran crimson down that cross, how many looked up at him and saw it as a *good* thing? When we read the redemption story, we see his blood as beautiful and holy; but at that moment, all they could see was red.

Sometimes God allows dreams to be dashed because *they are not his will.*

Maybe there was someone wonderful you thought you were going to marry, but minds were changed, and promises were broken. Your shattered heart may feel that the happiness has been lost forever. But you never know what God was saving you from.

Maybe there was a dream job in a city you loved that would have provided you twice the salary you have now. It might have seemed like the perfect fit, until the door slammed shut. Still, you don't know what God was protecting you from.

There is incredible uncertainty and difficulty in shifting paths, but also excitement and certainty knowing that God is having his way through you and in you.

In Genesis 6-9, Noah watched his entire world wash away before him as God led him to a land of cleansing and truth.

In faith, Abram parted with everything he knew and then God provided him with more than he could ever imagine.

An ordinary teenage girl was engaged to marry a man, settle down, and live a normal life until an angel appeared to her and told her she would become pregnant with the long-awaited Messiah. As a result, she became one of the most significant figures in biblical history: the mother of the Savior of the world, Jesus Christ.

If you could see the story of your life play out ahead of you and see how God plans to use you to touch other's lives, do you think you would settle for your own simple plans? You may have dreams of sweetness, of a life that is free from distress and sorrow . . . but that often means free from growth.

The dream of living in a beachfront city in a cute little home overlooking the coast sounds so much sweeter than a life of longing and pain, a life spent cutting your fingers on shards of glass as you gather the shattered pieces of your broken dreams and stretch bleeding hands out to the Maker. But at the end of the brokenness, there is restoration and redemption. Because of the wounds, there is a closeness to Christ, something we never would have had if we had stayed comfortable.

We often tie our identity to our plans; I know I did. Years ago, all I wanted to do was attend a sparkling university on the Central Coast, marry a beautiful tan surfer boy, and live in a magical city south of Pismo. When my family and I left that world for the Western city, I thought my dreams had ended. My life felt ruined. I felt broken and depressed.

So, I built something else. I thought seeing the world and having adventure after adventure would prove to be a life worth living. But again, those plans collided with the will of the Lord.

Regardless of what I planned, God determined that his will was going to be done despite my attempts to fulfill my own desires.

God wrecked my plans for my life and put them back together in a beautiful way. He's still putting the pieces together, like kintsugi art. My beautifully ruined life is becoming a story of fulfillment and purpose, with all things coming together just as my Father promised.

Two years ago, I wouldn't have found meaning, purpose, or beauty in what I am doing. I wouldn't have had the motivation to pursue what I am or even to call what I'm doing ministry.

But it is, and I do, because I know undoubtedly that this is where the Lord has led me. Maybe it's where I'll remain, or maybe he'll open another door to something completely different.

My heart was hard when we first settled into this world. I didn't want to love these people, and I didn't want to stay here. My life was supposed to pan out the way I'd always dreamed. How could it even remotely look like something I wanted in a dry little town filled with people so different from who I thought I was?

But at some point the message became clear: it's not all about me, after all.

It wasn't until a year after I began this book that its message truly began to resonate in my life. Maybe I was beginning to understand thankfulness. Maybe it was because an invasive pandemic made me realize how I had taken for granted the ability to reach people easily, before all the walls and boundaries. That unnerving experience awakened me to the reality that there was very little time to harvest souls. I needed to spend my time glorifying God, not living for myself.

I was sitting in the backseat of my brother's pickup one summer evening. Old guitars echoed from the dashboard. The windows were down. A river breeze cooled the air around us. All at once, I realized I'd come to love my little red-dirt town. It wasn't the kind of love romanticized by tumultuous, passionate waves and beachy shores. It wasn't the beauty of the town keeping me there; it was the people. Hours before, I'd soaked up the sun and dipped my feet in the river with a friend, and now here I was, driving the same gravel road with my brothers and sister. How many times had I driven it, listening to music, talking with my mom, house hunting with friends, or simply enjoying some alone time—dreaming of how much I wanted life to change?

But now, I didn't want life to change. I didn't even care if it did.

All at once, everything felt peaceful.

Conclusion

I can't recount exactly when it happened to me. It wasn't one of those mountaintop moments where I heard God's voice speak to me the way Moses did when he was standing on holy ground. It wasn't an overnight transformation, the kind Paul had when he was traveling the road to Damascus. It wasn't an immediate change like that of the bleeding woman who merely touched the hem of Jesus' garment as he passed through the crowd.

The process was slow, like a flower blooming. My heart was timid at first, but after some time, and the realization that change is necessary and even good, it began to open itself up to new things.

When we lived on the salty Central Coast, I used to stroll the monarch butterfly gardens in Grover Beach, where eucalyptus trees were filled with sleeping butterflies huddled in burgundy-black clusters on and in between branches. At the time, I thought all those delicate creatures started out as wormy little caterpillars that turned into a mess of goo inside a cocoon. Later I learned that butterflies don't form a cocoon (like moths do). They hibernate in a chrysalis—which is actually part of the butterfly—and then after several months, they emerge and grace the world with something completely different.

Change is a process. For me, that process still isn't finished, otherwise I would know all there is to know about God. I would have solved the mystery and understood myself completely because I understand him.

But I don't. My perceptions of God are being stripped away as I come to know him more fully, as I start to learn more about myself, who I am, and what I'm supposed to do.

Prothesis is about living our lives for him. It's about touching every soul we meet and making the most of every opportunity. It's about building relationships. Most importantly, it's about knowing Jesus so he can transform us into something not only more beautiful, but completely new. If we let him, he can use us to change the life of another person. Or two. Or a hundred.

The tunnel is still dark, but I know what's at the end.

In the spring of 2021, when the truth of what I was writing started to soak into my thoughts and resonate with my heart, I found myself starting to love my work and my life, and even my so-called purpose. Whether I had finally discovered it was somewhat of a mystery. Perhaps I'd learned the secret of contentment, or perhaps I was just learning to rest in his truth.

I sat on the front balcony of my parents' house. The Western town was cool for once. Winter had slowly formed into something between broiling and refreshing, where blooms felt safe enough to come out. It wouldn't last, but we were appreciating it while we had it.

In my lap was Randy Alcorn's *Heaven*. As I read, I thought about the breathtaking glory that awaits us. And the more I thought about heaven, the less I cared about making something of myself on this earth.

If heaven is our final destination, then this earth and this life are a practice test. If everything we do in this life is reflected in heaven, then I want to be living this life to the fullest for my Lord and Savior.

I think we forget the truth about heaven. All too often, our focus becomes fixated on the now; somehow we forget that this earth is more of a pre-life than anything. Who wants to live in a world where heartache and sin thrive and the next day or even the next moment isn't promised? All things loved will almost certainly come to an end.

We're too attached to this earth . . . but then again, maybe we're longing for heaven more than we realize.

When all I wanted to do was travel the world freely—whether it was hopping on a jet for an assignment to Greece or venturing out in a '70s hippie van-turned-home—I knew that I would never see this world the way I wanted to. And even if I took all the safety self-defense courses, my Rottweiler, and a shotgun, could I still enjoy every moment like I wanted?

Could I sleep under the stars in a desert without worrying about what's creeping in the vast beyond?

We want to swim with the creatures in the deep yet worry about what lies in wait below. We long for solace and solitude in fields of wild daisies yet return with forlorn nostalgia.

What if we could enjoy this immense universe in all its beauty and glory without worry? What if we could thrive in every relationship and not worry about loving people perfectly because we are no longer imperfect?

If that's what we want on this earth, we will always be disappointed because it will never happen.

But in heaven, it will.

Heaven is worth living and dying for.

If the focus is *heaven*, why would we try to achieve anything more on this earth besides loving God and people and making him known? Why would we try to find a purpose that barely breaks the surface of who we are?

Our purpose is to make him known. Our final destination is heaven. We are spiritual beings belonging not to this world, but to a beautiful, perfect world that is far better than anything we could ever find here (Phil. 3:20).

It's no wonder we often feel so out of place, so lost and confused. Our mission is not to achieve fame and glory, to feel settled and perfect. If we ever feel settled and perfect or reach a point where we believe all our growth is complete, then we have lost it. We are not supposed to become perfectly happy on earth.

Contentment is good. Joy is good. Resting is good.

Stopping is not.

We are to keep our hands stretched forth, reaching for Jesus, longing for heaven, and living for God. We can't lose focus on what is coming.

I don't know what hidden mysteries or sweet surprises may reveal themselves along the way.

But he is in me. *By him can I know me.*

Yahweh. I breathe him in and out. Yahweh. Yahweh.

Nearer you are to me than the very air I breathe.

I have found joy and fulfillment in what I do because I know with certainty that it's where I'm supposed to be *for now*. I can't pull a book of regrets down from the shelf, close my eyes, and try to imagine what my life would have looked like if I had made a different decision. We are here because this is where he has led us. Every step was ordained, and every breath is counted. If the hairs on my head are numbered, I know he is holding my hand as I walk and run and skip and crawl in the sunshine and the darkness and the barren wastelands. I can be content here because he brought me here. It may be four years; it may be forever. It could change in an instant.

I've learned not only to be content but to be overwhelmed with joy—a joy I never knew I could find and one I never saw coming.

The pain and uncertainty of the past has been washed away and made new by the promises of my Savior. He has given me a heart of flesh, a new meaning to what was once void of direction. Like the butterflies in the chrysalis, the metamorphosis was part of me, but it was him too. None of us is ever alone as we discover who we were created to be.

I haven't found myself in a career, a relationship, a city, or even another country.

I was there all along, simply because he was.

Acknowledgments

Little do we know how much else goes into a book besides what's written. It's not just the editing, processing, emails about optional book covers, and whether Monet or Van Gogh inspired the final product.

Underpinning the foundation of what turns a manuscript into a book are conversations that happen on a warm spring morning that transpire to inspire, prayers whispered to heaven for sustainability and boldness to share what needs to be said, and the hand-crafted lavender lattes in which we find comfort as we shuffle through the trenches of editing for what feels like the millionth time. These are just a few of the hundreds of ways people around me have upheld me as I've curiously muddled through this process.

My gratitude and appreciation extend beyond the individuals I'm naming—whether they realize it or not, they played a part in what came to be. But to name some of those names, I want to thank, from the bottom of my heart,

Rebekah Tyne McKamie, the first pair of eyes to sort through the mess of thoughts and ideas and bring clarity; Mike Valentino, who further beautified and purified the message (as well as gave me the courage to not give up in the pursuit); Cimber Cummings, for answering endless questions and being a cheerleader all the way through. You're a beautiful soul. To Samantha Cabrera, for seeing so much beauty in the broken and creating this ministry in which we get to partake (and the gorgeous book covers); we really are the lucky ones. To Madison Aichele, whose grace and prayers carried me through till the end. To Allana Walker and Lara d'Entremont, the beautiful editors, and the rest of the team at Calla Press, thank you from the bottom of my heart for your diligence in following through in this calling, for using your gifts and time to bring *Prothesis* to life. You all inspire me. And, of course, to Mom, Dad, Jackson, Riley, and Harrison for bringing humor, comfort, joy, and peace and being my safe place. Always. (Thanks for letting me write about you, even if you didn't know it at the time.)

Above all, none of this would have been possible without the gentle prodding, painful molding, always refining love of my Lord and Savior, who ever so softly placed the idea in my head years ago and, along the way, allowed me to discover for myself what purpose really was. Through this beautiful life, you have bestowed blessings and gifts that I have done nothing on this Earth to deserve, but I am so, so thankful. May this be an offering that you use to bring others to yourself.